A Light to Guide Us Home

Lynn Robinson

A Light to Guide Us Home
By Lynn Robinson

First Published 2017
Copyright © Lynn Robinson

ISBN-13: 978-1978473676

TEAMAUTHOR UK
Self-Publishing with you

DEDICATION

To my mum and dad, for always encouraging me to live
my life how I wanted to live it and always believing in me
no matter how daft it may have sounded.

FOREWORD

Sitting here now contemplating how this book came to be, I realise that this has been just another journey that God and the angels have wanted me to take.

If anyone had told me 10 years ago that I would be sitting here now, writing, I would have laughed. This isn't something I ever thought of doing, and I do mean ever.

I am quite ordinary and no different than anyone else, however, the difference between many people and myself is only one small thing: spirits got through to me with quite a bang!

When you read my story, you will come to appreciate that we are all spoken to and guided daily, but I understand that sometimes and maybe a large percentage of the time, we are simply not listening.

The angels are speaking to us every day, not just at certain times of the day but all the time. God is guiding us through his foot soldiers, the angels and spirits, whether it is our loved ones who have already passed or guides who have been assigned to us for our time here on Earth, it is they who are advising us. I don't believe that Mediums or Psychics are particularly 'chosen' because they are better than anyone else; I just believe that they are the ones who are listening.

I want to show you how spirits connect with you, how they are guiding you every day, each one of you. You can learn how to listen and watch for the slightest sign, which will lead you to a calmer, happier existence.

To say this book has been easy to write would not be true; it has been hard, but the whole-time spirits were here by my side, reminding me chapter by chapter about my life and showing me how they were connecting with me even as a small child. My life became calm and peaceful once I understood what was going on in my mind; I wasn't going crazy…I was hearing God's voice through his workers.

Within this book is the key to show you how to tap into your own divine guidance, your pathway to enjoying a better life and helping you manifest your dreams and wishes. You didn't pick up this book by mistake, you were guided; your guides have brought you to me and through me, they will speak to you.

I hope you enjoy my writings and the information brought to you from God and the angels. You are in the right place at the right time.

Enjoy your journey my dear friend, our souls will meet one day – of that I am certain.

ONE

My Journey to Medium-ship

When I first set out on my new journey of mediumship I asked again and again, 'why me'? Why have I been chosen to do this for others? Why can I receive these messages when others are struggling to do the same thing?

There were a lot of questions in the beginning, but it wasn't long before they were all answered. At first, it was difficult to hear clearly the messages that were given to me; I always could see the spirit there in front of me – I could describe hair colour, eye colour and many other things, including sometimes how they had passed and how old they were. I was always baffled as to how I could understand these things; I think I was trying far too hard. I was listening for clear voices, someone stringing a sentence together just as someone would hear when having a conversation with a friend.

I used to hear my guides telling me to look for the signs. 'What signs'? I would think and again I would listen, waiting desperately for a voice to speak clearly into my ear. This never happened more than a couple of times; it was on a rare occasion I would hear my name being shouted, 'Lynn, Lynn', I would hear, but there was not a soul in sight.

I began to piece the jigsaw together one tiny step at a time. I would have a sign for each of my loved ones in heaven. When I needed comfort or just reassurance that they were around me, I would look for the signs that we had agreed upon. I remember when I used to feel that my father had moved away from me, I couldn't feel his presence near me. Then one of the angels stepped forward and his words I will never forget. "Dear, once you have become accustomed to your father's energy, he is with you whenever you think of him, when you say his name or see his smile, he is there."

"I just cannot sense his energy however hard I try," I replied.

I heard a little chuckle, then he replied to me, "If your father was asked to step back from you just for even one day, you would feel the emptiness, or you would feel a hollow where he once was, then you would also realise that your father's energy has become a part of your daily life, just like your arm or your legs. If they were taken from you, there would be a huge sense of emptiness but every day you take the feelings of those limbs for granted, because they are simply just there."

I felt a sense of relief as I understood exactly what he meant; I would never doubt my loved one's presence again. My father and I have a bit of a game; when he is close by, I ask him to send over a small, one-man aircraft, the type he loved to fly. You don't see many of those where I live so it makes me smile when I see one fly quite low over my home.

These are the signs you are looking for with your own loved ones; make a pact with them. For instance, when I find a penny or when I see a feather or maybe a cheeky bird or a flash of light – you decide what it is and look for those signs every day. It brings a certain sense of relief when you start to realise that they are there with you and watching over you.

If learning about spirits and setting out to become a medium, you must first realise that with this comes a sense of responsibility. People will come to you looking for answers, looking for closure and sometimes their lives are in turmoil, trying to make sense of all their emotions.

You have a duty to be kind and thoughtful in the way you conduct yourself at your meeting. I have met a few mediums who have no filter system whatsoever! This can cause damage and pain to that person whom you are sitting with at that time. I feel there are unwritten laws which govern us to protect those who seek peace and closure in their lives.

We are chosen because we are people who care, and we are gentle in our manner; I believe that what has been given could as easily be taken away if we hurt others with our gift.

Prior to learning to contact the spirit world, we must truly know ourselves and how to recognise our own thoughts and emotions and learn how to differentiate them from any information coming in from the spirit world. There are many ways you can do this and it's the one that everyone who attends my classes always tells me they find the hardest. You must learn to sit quietly in meditation, to be at one with yourself. Once you learn to quiet your mind, you will have made room for the spirit world to step forward and communicate with you.

The aura, which is the light which surrounds your body, is the part of you that can connect you between two worlds and connect to other people's spirit, both in this world and the spirit world. It is an energy that radiates from our body and reflects our thoughts and feelings. Learn how to sense your own aura, and those of other people, by working beyond the senses which you have as a human. You can learn to connect with those who have passed over.

I feel we are governed by out spirit team, of which there are many. Everyone has a spirit guide – they are around us daily. Sometimes we have shown them in a dream or in quiet moments. I feel the different guides are with us to show us many different things during our lives. As with our guardian angel, our guide is with us from birth and stays with us until the day we are taken home. They are with us through thick and thin, helping us to make the right decisions and helping us to live a full life while we are here, which is such a short time within the whole picture of existence.

The development of your relationship with your spirit guide and your guardian angel is essential to developing fully with your mediumship. A sense of trust will grow and eventually you will not question what you are being given for any situation. There are times during development when you will question what is being given to you and what it is you are feeling. Don't worry, everyone goes through the same thing – hesitating before they make the move in the right direction. As with your loved ones, you can have a sign with your guides that they are there by your side; this helps you to test their presence and will help to reassure you that they are working with you.

Learning what you have been naturally given is not as hard as you think. In my next book, I will describe in detail how to make this fulfilling journey into peace and happiness.

I hope when you read my story you will see how spirits have contacted me since I was a tiny child and have helped deliver me to where I am today.

May you feel the love and energy within the pages of this book and may it help to bring you to where you naturally belong.

TWO

My Story

My medium-ship began with a heightened awareness as a young child; I used to see things in my room that frightened me to death! I spent most of my time crawling into bed next to my big sister telling her there was a monster in my room. However, it wasn't until my father died some 27 years ago that I realised what I was experiencing. For years I pushed these experiences to the back of my mind.

Since I have become enlightened, I have found that in my quiet moments and when I couldn't sleep, it was a relief to admit that the voices I was hearing were indeed spirits and that I wasn't losing my mind! In realising what it was I could hear, I started to sleep well for the first time in years!

Once I started to move forward on my spiritual path, life became more calm and welcoming. There were times in my life I would channel information for business colleagues, important information to help them move on with their business. I would do this without being aware of where this information was coming from. I worked in the corporate world for over 20 years and helped run businesses and give advice; I can now see this was clearly being channelled from spirits. I was called upon rather a lot by people and some abused this ability to help them move on with whatever it was they were doing at that time, only to leave me wondering what on earth had happened. I now recognise it was one of life's lessons I had to learn, and a lesson I learnt the hard way.

I would take telephone calls, which usually started out with the question, *what should I do'*? My guides would step in and tell them what to do, and give them ideas to help them move forward. I would then be promised the world in return for all this help. 'You are my right-hand woman', they would say. 'We can do this together'. Then of course, I was dropped like a hot rock and nothing I was promised ever materialised. Some of these life lessons were undeniably painful, and I was always drawn in by these people and believed their sincerity.

I have spoken to my guides and the angels who guide me daily and I asked why I was left to deal with this alone, and why these lessons were so heart-breaking. They would smile and tell me that these experiences were not just mine to learn, the people who had taken advantage also had lessons to learn. Some of them will never acknowledge these teachings in this life and will need to return again to correct what they have done wrong. They will be their own judges and jury on their return home. There is such a thing as Karma but it is different to what we think it is.

When you send love and light out into the world,

love and light will turn around and shine right back to you. When you do people an injustice or take from them without a thought of remorse, this too will come back to you, and this is what Karma is all about.

What we send out is like a boomerang, it will return and this is a very powerful thought. The message here is to remember that when you are unkind or hurt someone who cares about you deeply, then one day the same attitudes will return to you, without a doubt.

I decided to research more about what I was experiencing, and the more I researched, the more my guides displayed to me and the stronger my abilities became. My psychic gifts are now in constant demand with private readings, and I'm very honoured that I can bring peace of mind to so many of my clients. I am overwhelmed with the reviews my clients have written about their experiences with me, and there isn't a day that goes by that I am not grateful for all the support from spirits and the angels.

My spirit guides explained to me that I was a healer and the next move in my life should be to study Reiki. This has brought peace and calm to the lives of many and I am now a Reiki Master teacher. I feel there is a lot of good that I can do with what has been given to me, and I continue to learn more and more every day about this amazing life I now live.

I am very much a family lady and I have three lovely children, a stepson, and five grandchildren; to say I adore my family, is just not a big enough word to describe my feelings. I would move heaven and earth for all of them and sometimes with God's help it feels like I have done.

I am very fortunate to have a handful of very loyal

friends, some I have had since childhood, and although I don't always see them, we continue to be close and would support each other at the drop of a hat. I have made some like-minded friends on my journey who I consider to be a part of my extended family. I believe there is a lot of love to be given and received, and people will be placed in your pathway for your benefit. People also will be removed just as quickly if they are not good for your soul, in order that balance can be restored. Sometimes this can happen quite abruptly.

My father died when I was in my early 20's. I miss him dearly but he now is one of my daily guides; he watches over our family every day, still showing his support from up in the heavens. Whilst you read on in this book you will understand how support is given to you from your loved ones.

I would like to say a big thank you to our lovely mum Diane, who has been a constant support to me in the life I now choose. Mum never lets us down; she is always the first to say how wonderful we all are or indeed if we are not! Mum is now 82 years young; she loves her Reiki sessions with me and supports my work 100 percent. My childhood was a happy one and for this I feel truly blessed.

Working with spirits has become a lifetime purpose, and using my gift to help grieving families find closure. I was asked to write this book a few years ago but I just couldn't get my head around the fact that I would be writing; it just wasn't on my list of things to do; however, spirits are very persistent and believe me if something is a part of your journey, they don't give up!

The reason for this book, I am told, is to help

others out in the world to appreciate that this ability is given to every single one of us, not just a select few. We are all born with this skill; it was given to us before we came to be. I hope this book will help everyone out there who wants to connect to spirits and live a more comfortable, peaceful existence. I won't pretend that this will be easy, as with everything worth doing there is work involved. I wish you all love and light and with a little perseverance you too could be talking to your guides one day soon.

THREE

My Childhood

My awareness of spirit and the angels began as a young child; I would see things in my room that really scared me. It was the usual thing most young children experience, feeling frightened of the dark but not knowing why and thinking we see something out of the corner of our eye, and adults around me putting it down to an over-active imagination. All these things happen to most children, so why would I be any different? This was a question I would spend my life asking. I spent most nights in my early years crawling into bed next to my big sister telling her there was a monster in my room. I would see faces on the wall or a voice calling my name. I now know I was being spoken to by a divine presence, not a monster.

I now have 3 children and 5 grandchildren and most of them have experienced the same phenomenon I had as a child. I don't think my eldest son David believes; he looks at me as if I am nuts when I talk about spirits, but he did call on me once to help with a haunting in his home when his daughter was a very young child. I will write about my grandchildren and their experiences with spirits, and a haunting that turned out to be a beautiful story, later in this book.

It wasn't until my father died in 1989 that I realised what I was experiencing, and even then, it didn't really sink in. For years I pushed these experiences to the back of my mind.

Born in the sixties I was just a normal girl, but very quiet with a great love of animals from an early age. I grew up in a very loving and safe family environment, I am grateful for the memories of my childhood, and my hard-working parents set a wonderful example to my siblings and me.

Growing up having a very close bond with my parents and my three siblings was a blessing; we had a traditional family life. Mum and Dad were hard-working. Mum used to work as a nurse in the very old Leasowe hospital on the Wirral. Part of this hospital was used as a mental asylum, and my mum told us stories when we were growing up of the many deaths in the hospital. The hospital was known to be haunted and I would cringe at the thought of even entering the building, never mind working there.

The hospital was very close to the sea, literally within walking distance; some nights with the full tide my mother wouldn't make it home. She would be stranded unless she waded out to higher ground. As the high tide rose, so did the floods in the area. The water sometimes could be seen lapping at the foot of Cadbury's Hill. Some years later, the local council decided they would build a flood barrier which has held the tide back now for many years. When Mum left the hospital, she went on to be a cook in a nursing home, and that was to be her job for many years. In fact, she worked as a cook until the day she retired.

My mum was the strict one in the family unit; although she was firm, she had another side to her. She was also gentle and loving. I would say the 'perfect' mother; we never got away with giving cheek or backchat. I remember it well – if we were cheeky, our bottoms would sting for hours. This never did any of us any harm and we loved our mum dearly and still look to her for help and advice to this day, even though she is now in her eighties. She is a wise lady indeed.

The other side to Mum was very nurturing and loving; in my eyes, my mum was a superstar. She had a perfect balance of bringing children up with good manners and being well behaved. She would pride herself on the behaviour of her children and would always say and still does, "I can take you all anywhere without ever worrying, you were angels and always respected everyone around you."

I think there must have been times when Mum was so exhausted and she felt ready to drop! She would balance the family, her job, her husband, the housework and much more, and I don't ever remember her complaining. She has been an inspiration to us all, instilling hard work and family values deep within us. She continues to support us all; there is nothing you can't go and talk to mum about. She is a good listener and free with her advice, although sometimes she can be a little scary when she is cross, but we all love her dearly.

It was years later I would learn where my gift of

medium-ship came from. We would always joke and say, 'Mum must be psychic', as she always knew what was happening around her. We just accepted this as mother's intuition. Our lovely mum continues to be my biggest supporter, she encourages me with every step of my journey, and she comes to my house once a week and enjoys a Reiki session to ease her aches and pains, of which she has many.

My father was also a very hard working-man, I never knew him to be out of work for a day in his short life. My dad was my super hero. I loved him beyond words; he was the quiet parent, and when we were in trouble with Mum we would run to Dad and he would hug us and tell us everything was ok, and that Mum was just tired.

My father had worked every day of his life; one of his jobs was a bus driver but this was before I was born. When I was young, he worked with the Mersey Tunnel Police, I was so very proud that my dad was a policeman on the tunnel. I remember the day they opened the Queensway Tunnel and the Queen came to perform the ceremony. My dad managed to get us front row seats. There were lots of children from all over Merseyside who had come to watch the Queen cut the ribbon to the tunnel which created our new link to Liverpool and when the ceremony was over, the Queen came over to greet the children and onlookers and I gave her some flowers. What an exciting moment that was for me to touch the Queen…I felt like Cinderella. Children today wouldn't be impressed with the simple things that gave us such wonderful memories; it's a shame as life passes them by, with their heads in their computers and electrical gadgets.

I had very long blonde hair right down my back; Mum would wash it in the bath and send me downstairs with a towel wrapped around my head. I would sit on the floor and Dad would rub it dry. Sometimes he rubbed it so much it looked like a burst cushion, and you try getting a brush through that afterwards! This memory of my father still stays with me. It's strange, but I now struggle to hear my father's voice. I hear other people's loved ones daily, giving messages and connecting them to their family, but with my loved ones I find it quite hard to connect. At first, I didn't understand why this was so; I would be angry at spirits and God, asking them why this was so difficult for me.

Their answer, as usual, made sense. 'Your loved ones are now free Lynn, free of their human life and have moved into a different part of their existence. They are with you on this Earth approximately 50 percent of the time, showing their support and bringing love into your hearts. If you heard them as clearly as you hear us or others' loved ones, you would not move on in your life, you would be frozen in time, and long for them to be by your side. I know sometimes this brings you sadness, but you still have your life to live here on Earth. They can move around anywhere they wish; most of the time they are at the side of their loved ones, and sometimes they will become a guide but not very often. The reason for this is that they would guide you still with their hearts, and sometimes this is not what you need'. My guide would tell me that sometimes we need someone to be firm with us and bring us sharper advice. 'Know Lynn, that they are around you, and they still love you as they did in life'.

This message from my guides brought a greater understanding of how they communicate with us. I feel very blessed to have such wonderful teachers.

The one thing I didn't like during my childhood was anyone smoking around me, however this was very fashionable then, and my dad smoked like a chimney; I believe this contributed to his early death some years later. I used to hate the smell of cigarettes, in fact I always blame them for my travel sickness, we would go on holiday to Anglesey and I would suffer the whole 100 miles!

During this time, heaven and the angels where showing me things I didn't understand. I just thought I had a very vivid imagination. My dad would talk to me, telling me of God and Jesus and the angels, and how they would help me if I ever needed them, and how there was this wonderful place where we all would go when we died, a place where everyone is happy and everyone knows love. I used to stare at him thinking how wonderful this all sounded, and how clever my dad was for knowing all this these things about heaven and God. He would inspire me to think of the angels, and I think this is why I had my head in the clouds for so much of the time.

When Dad talked about these things, I could feel myself being lifted higher and higher, I didn't want him to stop. My father was very spiritual and believed totally there was a heaven; God and his angels are waiting for all of us to take us home on our day of passing.

My brother Steve, who is the eldest of my siblings, joined the Merchant Navy when I was young. I remember his long trips away only to be laced with excitement on learning he was due to return. He travelled the world and was able to see many countries in his young life. He would return laden with gifts from Africa and beyond. I never had a proper sister/brother relationship with him as he was always away, but when he was home, it felt like all our Christmases had come at once.

The bond between us has never broken and I don't remember there ever being any harsh words between us. I love him dearly and always will, and no matter what happens, come hell or high water, we will always be there for each other till our very last breath, in that I have no doubt.

My brother married a local girl; she came from a large family, and is a very private person. She was always very spiritual and God was a big part of everyday life. My brother and his wife have three children, two boys and a girl, and I remember when their first son was born I was overjoyed, my first nephew – what a gift. Their daughter grew up with the same love of horses as I had and we have always had a special bond between us both.

I also have an older sister Janet; she is seven years older than I, and there are many fond memories of summers with my sister when I was very young. We used to walk over the railway bridge and go to the beach. We were so lucky to live by the sea. It was empowering and still is to this day. We would walk down the country lanes past all the farmers' fields and the pigs in their pigsties, and then we would go and pick our own strawberries. When I look back, life was so much simpler for children then and all those little things meant such a lot.

There was a house which I used to love; it looked like it didn't belong on the lane where it stood, as all the other houses where very old farm houses and barns. This bungalow looked Spanish. It was white and gleaming with beautiful ranch fences and the best thing about it were the horses in the field; how I loved the horses – they took my breath away, so majestic and elegant. I loved every inch of them, every flowing hair, the look in their eyes as if they knew exactly what I was thinking. It was then that I fell in love for the first time, and many years on I am still in love with my horses. I used to dream I would live there; little did I know that this house would be the first gift from the angels.

My sister Janet would sleep in the smaller box room in our family home, but there would be many nights she would be awoken by a terrified little sister: me! 'Please can I sleep with you, there is a monster in my room', I would cry as I entered her room. It got to the point when she would hear the door open and when I reached the bed she had already moved over to let me in, and not surprisingly, many years on Jan would be one of my biggest supporters in my spiritual awakening.

My parents and sister dismissed what I was seeing at a very early age – they thought it was my vivid imagination! I would see faces in my room, monsters so I thought! I was never a very good sleeper; my mind was so active and I could have written a story with what was going on in that head of mine. What I didn't appreciate was those voices; those ideas, that conversation was spirits and not some over-active imagination of a 5-year-old.

In the late sixties, my younger sister Cathy was born. I remember it was getting close to Christmas and my mum and dad used to say that there would be a new baby for Christmas; I don't mind telling you, a baby wasn't on my Santa's list! My mum was taken into hospital just before Christmas, and on December 22nd my little sister was born. I was not impressed; I wanted my mum and I missed her. Mum stayed in hospital all over Christmas, much to my disgust. Luckily, I had a lovely nan and granddad, my dad's parents, and they lived just across the park from us. We all went to their house for Christmas dinner and I recall a story Mum told me of our visit to the hospital to see her and the new baby. Mum asked me, "What did you all have for Christmas dinner?" She said I was so upset at not having her home that I replied, "We had stew!" Poor Nan had cooked a lovely Christmas lunch with all the trimmings; it was just not the same without our mum there.

I always loved Christmas dinner; even now it's the best part of Christmas. Dad has been gone over 27 years now, and Mum stills comes to us for her Christmas lunch most years since he died. These times are precious; we won't have her forever, Dad will come and take her home before we know it and I will always have these memories to look back on. When Dad was so ill he would talk to me about his passing; I hated this as of course, we didn't want to lose our dad. His last request to me was, "Lynn promise you will look after Mum for me."

Of course, this went without saying, and I like to think that over the years Dad has been gone, I have done my very best for Mum. She has lived with me twice both times when she was very ill and needed constant care. For 20 years after my father passed, on every family holiday we would count a place for Mum. I know my mum always loves and appreciates all I have done, and I hope over all these years she never felt lonely, and I feel happy knowing my father's last wishes were delivered as promised.

I loved visiting my grandparents; Granddad was a funny man. He used to make us laugh with his stories. He had lost his leg in the war from above the knee and so had a wooden leg. I always remember he used to joke with me telling me to scratch his foot for him as it was itchy and then he would knock on his leg as I did it and make me jump. Granddad loved his rose garden and it was his pride and joy; he used to let me dead-head the roses and my nan would show me how to make perfume out of the fallen petals. I can still smell those roses now. They were lilac/blue in colour and the smell was just heavenly. Unlike the perfume that I had made from the fallen petals, I felt we didn't have granddad long. He had a bad heart and he passed over to the angels when I was very young and that was my first encounter with death.

My nan was just fabulous! I loved everything about her; I always remember she used to make us crumpets and hot Ovaltine – those were the days; I just loved my visits. My nan was very lonely when granddad passed, she stressed quite a lot about being on her own in the house. So much so that my brother Steve moved in with her so that she wouldn't be alone. I remember it was around this time that my brother had left the Merchant Navy and had joined the local fire department. I was very proud that my brother was a fireman, and made sure I told everyone I encountered. There was one thing my nan was terrified of and I never understood as I grew up to love it, but she was terrified of the storms – thunder and lightning. We lived across the park from Nan, so it took 5 minutes, running to get to her house. As soon as we heard the first rumble, my mum would say, 'Quickly, go to Nan's she will be under the table'!

It wasn't until I grew up that I learned it wasn't the storms Nan was frightened of but the loud bangs of thunder and the cracks of the lightning…after all, she had lived through two world wars. My mum used to say it was the angels in heaven bowling; I would stay the night with my nan to keep her company while my brother was on the night shift. Those visits are memories that will stay with me for eternity. How I miss my trips to my lovely grandmother's. Her hugs and her stories have been a part of my life and have stayed with me always. Nan would tell me of the war days and how even though food and most things were in short supply, they were always happy, and everyone helped everyone else. No one would stand by and watch a neighbour go without. The community was strong and people really cared about each other.

When she passed, my mother and father kept a very old display cabinet of hers, in which she used to keep her best china. My mother has since given it to me as she has no room in her flat and she said I was so close to Nan and always loved the cabinet, it should be mine. If I close my eyes and open the door, it sweeps me back to my childhood, and to this day that cabinet still smells the same.

My younger sister Cath I feel just grew up before my eyes! I say this because I don't seem to remember her as a baby as those years went by so fast. My memories of Cath were during the family holidays, we used to spend our holidays on Anglesey with our parents; those were some of the happiest days of our lives, apart from the journey there and back with my head out of the window! We had a caravan on this magical island. I loved it beyond words, and it was such an adventure. Our caravan was on a big site set in woodland not far from Llygwy Beach; the adventures we had were amazing, our search for fairies in the woods, paddling in the icy stream, our play times were endless.

I wasn't a very girly girl, although you wouldn't have thought so to look at me, long curly blonde hair, big blue eyes, but Wellingtons and mud fitted with me so well. It was there in the quiet of the island I would hear some of my first messages from the angels. I didn't know what the voices were at the time nor the messages I was receiving. I only know this today because my guides remind me of my early life with spirit. My parents thought that I was a very sensible girl and always kept my little sister and myself out of trouble, however I now know it was my angels telling me to be careful. 'Don't do that' or 'Don't go down there', they would guide me. 'You might get stuck', they would say. Mum would say I was like a mother hen, the way I took care of my little sister. My bond with Cath has never broken; she grew up to be a highly respected member of the local community and has continued to serve the community the same way for over twenty-five years. I am a very lucky lady indeed to have this bond with my family.

One night, Mum and Dad had nipped up to the little club on the site, which was very close to our caravan. Cath and I were in bed and were told not to leave the caravan, but that night was one of my early sightings of spirits. I could see a shadow on the wall and it started to move towards my sister. I was terrified of the shape – it looked like a great big hairy spider, probably two feet across. The shape told me not to be frightened, yet I was terrified. It looked similar to the shape I saw on my bedroom wall at home.

Carefully, I woke my little sister and we put on our Wellington boots and then proceeded to find Mum and Dad. It makes me smile now because I left the safety of the caravan and walked in the pitch black up to the top of the caravan site – what could be scarier than that? When we reached the top, I looked at the clubhouse and a voice in my head told me that Mum would be cross as I promised I wouldn't leave the caravan. So, I decided to go to one of my parent's friends' caravans instead. Meanwhile, Mum and Dad had left the club and walked back down to our caravan only to find their girls had gone! We could hear Mum scream from the top of the site and needless to say I never went wandering alone again and my parents never left us alone again. As for the shadow man and the voices which I had clearly heard, again, my parents told me I had a vivid imagination. My guide Angel Raoul has told me that the sighting of this large spider was bringing me knowledge; I can't help thinking, could they not have found a less terrifying method of delivery?

Our first family home, I remember, was most definitely haunted without a doubt and still is to this day! The house was always freezing cold no matter what Mum and Dad did, sometimes you could see your breath. It didn't help that there was no such thing as central heating. I can remember not wanting to get out of bed in the morning to go to school, and just wanted to stick my head under the cover and hide!

I would hear voices on the top landing of the house, the family bathroom was right at the top of the stairs. As I stepped out of the bathroom, I would feel a presence on the stairs and it would be a frightening experience. I don't know how I didn't fall from the top to the bottom many a time trying to run away from this manifestation. At first, I would feel the cold rise up behind me, and then there was a rush as if someone had just run up the hallway right behind me. I would see what seemed like a black shadow of a very tall man. This awareness was quite a strange sensation, I would close my eyes, terrified so that I wouldn't see it, but this actually didn't help and all it did was give me a clear vision in my head of what he looked like. He was a very tall figure, I would say around six feet. He was dressed all in black, a bit like the headless horseman we've seen in films. I felt he wore a very long cloak, and looked as if he wasn't from our century; I was so frightened it took my breath away.

Looking back now and after being given these memories from Raoul my guide, I do believe the ghost was stuck in the house. I now know he was from the same century as the ghost who lived in the house where I now live and he too was a big part of the smuggling ring that was happening off the shores of Wirral, many centuries ago.

I will tell you this story later in my book, as this forms part of another haunting experience!

FOUR

My Gifts from the Spirit World

I have come to understand that all my experiences were something called clairsentience, which means clear sensing, and is the ability to feel the present, past or future as well as the physical and emotional state of others, without the use of the normal five senses. Indeed, I had been physic my whole life. One of my first experiences that I remember, or should I say that the spirits have reminded me about, is about my brother whom I mentioned earlier. Steve was in the Merchant Navy and travelled all over the world. I had not long started my first school at around 5 years of age. I had broken down in the playground and I was crying inconsolably. One of the teachers came over to me and asked what was the matter; I couldn't breathe, all I kept saying was he is dead he is dead! They took me inside and called my parents.

My mum came to school to find out what on earth was going on. In my mind, I knew something was wrong with my brother, I just couldn't figure out what. I was taken home, Mum asking, "What on earth is wrong with you? I had to be called out of work!"

I was distraught; I kept saying over and over, 'he is going to die'. I was told it was all nonsense and put in my room. I must have fallen asleep as later that evening I awoke to hear my mum crying. I crept to the top of the stairs to listen, which believe me was not my favourite place in that house! I heard my mother sobbing. I could barely pick out what she was saying, but I knew it had something to do with my brother.

I found out that he was out at sea not far from China. He had been in terrible pain and they realised it was his appendix. The pain had got worse overnight and he was in a bad way. He was airlifted to Mainland China and nearly lost his life, as his appendix had burst. He underwent emergency life-saving surgery, and was going to have to stay in China for a week or so. What had happened to me in school was never mentioned or linked to this event, but I now realise on being asked to write this book by my guide and Angel Raoul, that I had been witnessing, or some might say forecasting, this life-threatening situation as it was happening to my brother.

There were lots of similar situations through my early years; I had a sense of perception so that I was constantly careful as I knew something bad could happen. The angels talked to me constantly and were protecting me; I sometimes would hear messages as they guided me to safety every day.

I always had this love of animals from a very young age, my heart just melted at the thought of a cuddle from the cat. I really wanted a horse; their grace and presence just overwhelmed me. I would go to the RSPCA and help as a young child. I was too young to go alone so I would go with a neighbour who was older than me, and she would look after me on the bus. I loved visiting, but all the dogs in those cages made me feel very sad. I just wanted to let them out, to set them free.

A lot of dogs and cats would be on death row, as they used to call it. It was so upsetting. We would be allowed to walk the caged dogs and give them some love and care. I used to regularly walk the five miles home with a dog due to be euthanized, and plead with my mum to agree to keep him/her as they were going be put to sleep. The tears would pour down my face, as I begged for this animal's life. My mum would be at her wits' end with me, sadly, to the point where she had to stop me from going. I always had this connection with the animals; they seemed to understand me and I them. Just imagine if Mum had let me keep every dog and cat – we would have been overrun with animals.

I continued to be drawn to the animals and after going to the RSPCA daily and sometimes twice a day during the school holidays, I accepted that animals were going to become a large part of my life. I do think that people thought I was a little bit batty because I often said I could hear them talking to me. I knew what they wanted and when they were in pain; I just knew they needed love and some cuddles.

When I think about it now, this meant that I was destined to never be alone in my life as I would always have my animals by my side and that the love and bond between us would be endless until the day I take my last breath, of this I have no doubt. It's only now that I am being reminded of these times that I really know that, again my voices, my guides and the angels had sent me to help these beautiful souls to show them love and caring before they went home to God and the angels.

I work every day now with spirits and my guides are leading me constantly. I have many bookings in my home for spiritual readings and I have confirmation that all of God's creatures go to heaven, as they have visited me and their loved ones during my work. This brings great comfort and healing to all the people who visit me looking to connect with their loved ones.

This is an email review, which was sent to my Facebook page some time ago from a lady who was connected to her beloved dog during a reading.

My reading with Lynn:

I know some people might think I am crazy, but my big softy Alex was a huge part of my life. You see, I had been in an aggressive relationship, and my Rottweiler Alex was a puppy when this all started. He would cower in the corner terrified, while the verbal and sometimes aggressive beatings were taking place. As he grew, so did his protective instinct for me. It wasn't long before he started to bark at my ex-husband as if to warn him off. One day when Alex was just one year old, my ex came home after a night in the pub. He dragged me out of bed by my hair; Alex always had to sleep downstairs and wasn't allowed in the bedroom. Something told me never to shut him in a room, so I bought some child gates, and Alex slept behind one of them. On this night, I thought my ex would kill me – my life flashed before me. I am not usually a person who hears spirits, but a voice in my head was saying, 'Alex, Alex'. I screamed to Alex and I heard a thud. He had cleared the child safety gate and was on his way up the stairs. He burst through the door, launching at my ex-husband, bringing him crashing to the floor. My husband wondered what had hit him! I was frightened for Alex but something made me stay calm. Alex put himself between my aggressive husband and me!

It all happened so quickly, Alex attacked again, pinning my husband to the floor. I was shouting to the dog now, hoping he would not go too far, as it would bring my horrible husband great pleasure to have Alex put to sleep for being dangerous. Suddenly, it seemed to go quiet in the room. The only thing between me and another beating was my lovely dog. What happened next was amazing; my husband stood up, threw his hands in the air, and told me neither of us were worth the hassle. He turned and walked away and I never saw him again. My Alex had saved me, I believe, and he loved me unconditionally. I never saw this side of Alex again. He was gentle and loving and everyone loved this gentle giant of a dog. He saved my life without a doubt. It was the saddest day of my life when Alex was old and could no longer go for our walks and the day had come I had to let him go. I was heartbroken to say goodbye to my beautiful dog.

I came to Lynn for some Reiki healing which I have to say was amazing. I have been to so many healers before and never felt the benefit of what I received that day. Lynn certainly has healing hands amongst many other gifts from God.

After the healing, Lynn sat me down to talk over everything with me. Suddenly, we heard what seemed to be crackling or something like that. Lynn looked at me and said, "I have a very strange question for you Donna, have you lost a dog to spirit, a big dog, brown and cuddly?"

I looked at her with tears in my eyes, "Yes I replied."

"Well, he is here," she said. "He is the crackling we can hear." I looked at her in amazement. "He is with a lady, dark hair, blue eyes, who tells me she is Mum." I gasped!

"Mum tells me your lovely dog is ok. He runs in the fields of heaven every day, and of a night, he sits by my fireside with me to keep me company. Let go of the pain my lovely girl," she said to me. I am fine and so is he. We are happy and at peace. You must get another puppy, you have a lot of love to give to another dog, and there are lots out there looking for homes just like you have to offer."

Then the most amazing thing happened – Lynn continued to speak. "I was there with you that terrible evening, Donna, I was there in spirit. I was the calm in the room; I tried so hard to keep your husband calm but he had the devil in him! You are safe now, live your life. There is new love for you, and you have wasted many years hiding from it." My mum told Lynn all about what happened that terrifying night.

The tears rolled down my face! I have never had such a connection to my mother. She described her perfectly, and the words Mum would use came out in the message. I have another puppy now and she is quite a handful. Sometimes she does the weirdest of things, when she is playing in the garden; she bounces and chases something around and around. I do believe this is my beloved friend Alex. I can't thank

Lynn enough. She has brought peace and love back to my life. Knowing that my loved ones are safe and I will see them all again someday helps me to move on and be happy. Thank you Lynn so very much from the bottom of my heart. You are a special lady with a loving and caring way and I will carry your words in my heart until the day I am taken by those angels you talk about so freely.

With love, Donna xxxx

It was such a pleasure to help Donna with her healing; I do believe that for many people a reading is the first step to really starting to recover after the death of a loved one. It is no coincidence when someone decides to visit a medium. It is spirit and the angels letting them know it is time for them to move on with their life, by guiding them to our doors and giving a medium the opportunity to comfort and offer consolation in starting the healing process.

I do believe that this review was given to me whilst writing this chapter for a reason. You see I too, have big dogs. My German Shepherd is called Zoey and she is 13 years old, my Rottweiler is a big bear of a dog called Max, and he was 12 years old at the time. Three days after I received this review for my website, my old boy Max, who had been struggling with his arthritis for 12 months, took a turn for the worse. Sadly, the vets told me there was nothing they could do for him; he was in a lot of pain. I had a big decision to make on the spot. I called on my dad and all my family that had passed to come and take my lovely boy home. We were broken-hearted as a family, and as I write it's only been five days since we lost him. We are all still very sad; he was faithful and bold and loved us all without doubt. Of course, I now know he is running in the fields of heaven with all my animals that passed before him.

For my dear faithful old friend Max, we will always have you in our hearts; come back and say hello sometime. Love you always xxxx

I often remember as a child I used to plead with my mum and dad to buy me a pony, and they would look at me with sadness in their eyes. Little did I know how expensive ponies were, and after 40 years of having horses, I now understand why they had that look upon their faces every time I asked. My dad used to say to me, "One day Lynn, I will win the pools and you can have the perfect pony and you'll be very happy,"

Well, as far as I can remember, my dad never won the pools, but they must have saved and saved and during this time. While I was taking my riding lessons, they bought me my first pony. I think this was when I was around nine years old. I will never forget that day as long as I live. We turned up at the riding stables and there he was, my favourite pony Dougal, and he was waiting for me. It was a stormy Saturday morning and I would usually get the bus with Sue my friend who lived in our street. Mum and Dad decided that they would come to watch me that wintery Saturday morning.

On arrival, Dad asked that I waited with Mum. This wasn't the usual way that things were done, I thought. The lady that owned the riding stables had the ponies tied up ready for the riders to arrive. My dad told me to wait with Mum while he spoke to her. She turned and smiled at me. I smiled back, wondering what was going on. We just usually lined up ready to lead our ponies into the arena. I heard a soft voice say, 'Patience Lynn, patience'.

One of the girls who rode with us on our lesson every weekend came over to me and whispered, "Lynn, Dougal has been sold and this will be the last time that you get to ride him. His new owners are coming to collect him." My stomach turned over, I felt so emotional. I loved this pony and I would miss him very much.

Dad continued his conversation with the lady and in the next instant the pony I always loved to ride was handed to my dad. Dad turned and walked towards me. He put the lead rope in my hand and then to my surprise he said, "He's yours Lynn, he is all yours." I looked at my mother and then father with tears in his eyes, I could not believe it. It was a dream come true. "A pony of my own, is this true?" I was so excited I cried with joy. I would never ask for anything else from them ever again. They had made my life complete, and at the age of nine, that was incredible.

It was a terrible day – the wind was blowing and the rain was battering down, but I didn't care, I took my pony out into the fields and loved every minute. That was one of the most memorable days of my life and I will never forget it as long as I live. Little did I know that 40 years later I would still have a horse of my own and that they would play such a big part in my life and my spiritual awakening. These horses were a gift from God and the angels to help me along the course of my life and the journey so far has been amazing.

FIVE

My Younger Years

In my younger years when Mum and Dad would go to work and during the school holidays I was so very fortunate to be looked after by two people whom I loved dearly. They used to live over the road from us, I knew them as my Auntie Doreen and Uncle Andrew. They were not blood relatives but they somehow felt like it.

I loved going to stay with them; they used to treat me like a princess and I loved every minute of the day, it was fabulous. I would put curlers in Aunty Doreen's hair and help with the garden. Those days were just wonderful. I felt sometimes I had two mums. Uncle Andrew would tell me stories about the place he used to live; he was a broad Scotsman and I loved the stories he told me about Scotland. The islands where he lived were called the Shetland Islands. The stories of the little ponies that lived on the Island, amazed me with the tales he would tell of their strength and how they would work the land, and how life used to be so simple, and all the nice little cottages dotted all over the island. It sounded just like something from a story book, quite magical.

He was such a wonderful storyteller, he would speak about a place in Scotland that would disappear at night behind the fog and then during the day in the sunshine this village would come to life; you could see the streets and houses, the children and the people. There would be stags in the garden and deer were all over the town; it sounded like such an enchanted place and I would sit there enthralled thinking one day I would love to visit.

It wasn't until years later that I recognised that he was telling me a bit of a tall tale as there was a film called Brigadoon and that was the story he was relaying to me, but I did love to hear him describe it all to me. Uncle Andrew has been to me a few times over the past two years, with messages of love for his family; also, he has been to guide me when I have needed family support from spirits. I like to picture him and my dad sitting around a log fire somewhere in heaven putting the world to rights.

My Auntie Doreen used to let me sit behind her chair and play with her hair. She would put a milk crate on the floor for me to stand on, I would play for hours with her hair putting it in curlers. I felt quite the little hair dresser. How I loved to do this! If you saw the state of her hair when I finished, you would wonder why she ever let me near.

She would tell my mum that I was a good girl and that I was a pleasure to have, I had good manners and was a joy to look after. I would love the days when I went over there to visit, as they had a daughter called Susan and she appeared to take me under her wing.

She had a little sports car – an MG soft top, and she would take me out in this car with the top down, and the wind-in-my-hair feeling was just fantastic. What a lovely life I had growing up; I was so very fortunate to have such special people around me.

Aunty Doreen would tell me that there were fairies at the bottom of her garden and this is why all the flowers were so beautiful. She would show me the flowerbeds, I think they were dahlias, maybe big daises and she would tell me that she didn't need to touch these flowerbeds she said that at night when we go to sleep the fairies would come out and tend the beds; they would sprinkle fairy dust so my flowers were beautiful colours. No I recall it spirit placed very spiritual people in my pathway, making sure that my love of God and the Angels was always instilled in my tiny mind.

I never found school particularly easy; in fact I found it awful – I never wanted to go. I would try and find an excuse why I shouldn't be there. I tried all the usual things, *I have a sore throat, I have a cold, I feel sick*, etc. However, this all used to backfire on me. My mum would say, 'If you're too ill to go to school, you can't go to see your pony'. So, I had to grin and bear it. There was nothing else for me to do.

I would spend most of my day with my head in the clouds. I was in the middle school now and mum said I had to buckle down. I tried, I really did, but I never seemed to be able to concentrate; my mind was filled with my pony and what I would do that evening when I arrived to see him. I never asked for much because I had my pony and on Christmas or my birthdays I would usually ask for something the pony needed and

I would be very happy as I really wasn't bothered about things for me.

I would have a new pair of Wellingtons or a new raincoat; the pony was all I ever wanted so *things* meant nothing at all. I didn't have many nice clothes as I spent most of my time in Wellingtons and jodhpurs. So, on that day when one of my friends asked me to come to the school disco, I was horrified. "What will I wear, Mum?" I asked.

"You can borrow a top from your sister and wear it with jeans." I felt gorgeous! Mum helped me with my hair and gave me a squirt of her perfume. Wendy, my friend, came to meet me at the corner of the street and we went to school together; it was great – the atmosphere was buzzing. This was my first disco and I already loved it.

I was never very interested in boys, I thought they were annoying, however, there was this particular boy and he used to look straight past me. I thought I would never be good enough for him. He was going out with this girl in school; she was everything I wasn't: fashionable, pretty and she had a boy who fancied her. On the night of the disco, that voice was in my head again, 'Go say hello, Lynn'. I was shy and afraid he would laugh at me. My voice pushed and pushed until I did. I said 'hello' to this handsome boy. With dark curly hair and very blue eyes, he was dreamy. At this time the film Greece with Olivia Newton John and John Travolta had hit the cinema. I loved this film and I thought this boy in school looked just like John Travolta. Looking back, I now think that rose tinted glasses must have been a part of the outfit I wore that night too.

His girlfriend noticed me saying hello to him. She

walked over and said hello, and I thought I was 'in for it' and with her friends behind her, they started to giggle! They laughed at the way I was dressed – they were being mean. She said to her boyfriend, whose name was Mark, "Go on, I dare you, give her a kiss. Make her day!" I blushed and went to walk away. She grabbed my arm and in an instant, Mark leant forward and gave me a kiss. I was all of a flutter; I didn't know what to do with myself, they were all giggling at me and I just wanted to go home, so I got my coat and left. They had ruined my night and I was very upset.

The next day I had to go into school. I certainly didn't want to as I knew they would all make fun of me and I felt a fool. A voice inside my head said, 'It's ok Lynn, go to school everything will be ok'. I reluctantly left home and headed down the road. I avoided everyone and kept my head down most of the morning. Lunchtime was another matter; I was in the lunch line when I heard a voice say, "Hi where did you run off to last night?"

I turned around and there he stood. I wanted the Earth to open up and swallow me! The voice in my head was telling me to take a deep breath and that all is well and to talk to him. I didn't know at this time that the voice I heard where my guides and the angels. I just assumed it was me and that I talked to myself a lot. I very bravely said, 'Hi, sorry I had to be home early'. I didn't dare tell him I had run home like a scared cat. Mark sat with me at lunch and all I could think was, 'Oh my goodness, they are tormenting me'.

I looked around for the giggling girls but no one was in sight. Mark told me that he liked me and would I like to go out with him. I looked at him with complete shock, "Me!" I proclaimed.

"Yes you," he laughed. "Why not?" he asked. "I really like you and I would love for you to be my girlfriend." I was amazed and flattered a boy had just asked me to go out with him. 'Dear Lord', I thought. 'What will mother say'? I was only 12 years old.

Oh, how I loved Mark. He would come to the horses with me and help me with my chores. I met his mum and dad and I felt they were such a lovely family. I now know that Mark had been put in my life for a very big reason, and that reason was to become clear one day.

We stayed together as girlfriend and boyfriend for a few months. We loved being together, and I just loved it that Mark liked my pony. It was time for us both to leave our middle school and go off to secondary school. We drifted apart at this time as we were both sent to different schools. Mark went to a boys' only school and I went to a mixed school. I think the circumstances and the different schools took us both in different directions as we split up and both met different people.

I have a friend called Helen. She also had a pony – our ponies were best of friends and so were we. We met at the riding stables, where we kept our horses. That was some 40 years ago and to this day she is truly the best friend I have ever had, she is my soulmate. God put us together for a lot of reasons. People consider their soulmate to be their husband, wife or indeed a great love. This is often very true, however, your soulmate can also be a great friend, one with whom you might have shared many things together, never judging, always helping. If you think about it, this is true love.

I loved staying at Helen's house. She lived in a

huge house in Wallasey with her brothers, her dad and step-mum. I used to stay most weekends and then we would go to the riding stables and stay there for hours. The voice in my head would tell me Helen was special like me and that we would be friends for the rest of our lives.

Helen had a brother who was also called Mark. He quite fancied me, and we started to go out together for a while. I think I was 13 or 14 when we met but Mark was older than me and he was going to leave school and go to college as he wanted to be a ship's captain. Our relationship was short lived but I always have fond memories of him. I met up with the other Mark again sometime after Helen's brother and I had split up; we fell straight back in love again.

I tried so hard to work in school but was always distracted. I wanted to leave to go and see my pony. I would hear one of my guides saying to me, "Come on Lynn, you're never going to finish. Get your head out of the clouds – you will get into trouble." I always listened and most of the time took notice of what was whispered to me. My guides knew me well and constantly tried to keep me on the right pathway.

On one particular day, a very strange occurrence happened as I arrived home from school. Mum was in a hurry. "I am going out with the girls from work," she muttered. "Will you put tea out, Lynn?" she asked. "I need to leave, tell your dad I won't be long." And with that, she rushed out the door. I only found out 2 years later exactly where mum had gone that night. She had gone to see a medium, a lady from Moreton. This lady told mum that she was going to get a shock – her daughter Lynn, would get pregnant!

She told Mum this wasn't going to go down very

well, as I was young and that I would need a lot of support. "What a load of rubbish," my mum told her, and walked home in a daze. I was 15 at the time of mum's reading, so she wasn't impressed with what this lady had told her. Nevertheless at the age of 16 I was indeed expecting. I was so ill, I thought I was dying; I had the dreaded morning sickness, which lasted morning noon and night! Mum took one look at me and knew that what this medium had told her was in fact happening. I was taken to the doctor's and it was announced to my mum that undeniably I was pregnant, and 12 weeks pregnant to be exact!

My mum was in shock. I was terrified that my dad would be so cross with me. "What are we to do?" Mum muttered. "This is terrible!"

I was sent to my room instantly and was told to await my father arriving home from work. I was terrified of what my dad would think of me. I sat and cried for hours, then it came – that knock on my bedroom door. The voice in my head told me that it would be ok and to open the door. I opened the door and there stood Dad. He looked at me, put out his arms and said, "Don't worry, we will work this out; we love you Lynn, now don't worry." Afterwards I must have fallen asleep on the bed, as when I awoke, it was morning.

We had to face Mark's parents and let me tell you that didn't go quite so well. Mark's mum was distraught; she piled the blame onto me. I had ruined her son's life; he was due to join the navy and his first trip was to the Falklands'. My angels were talking to me daily by now. I thought I was going nuts. 'It will be ok Lynn, don't you worry'. They seemed to tell me that all the time. Mark's mum and dad went to see the navy recruitment officer and told him what had happened. Of course throughout all this, his mother shouted that I was to blame for all of this...Mmm, I do remember her son having some part in it!

Mark had already been given his ship and the training had begun. My guides would tell me that all was working out as it should. It didn't feel like it, everything was going wrong. Mark's mum insisted this baby was to be 'got rid of', as she put it. I was marched to the doctor's, not my own doctor but their own family doctor; my voices were telling me this isn't safe, I was scared stiff!

Somehow Mark's mum had convinced everyone that the best thing to do would be to abort this child. They were arranging it with their doctor; I was being sent to Brighton for an abortion. Why was no one listening to me – I didn't want this to happen! But my parents weren't hearing my cries. I had an appointment with Mark's family doctor that evening. When Mum and I arrived, I could hear my voices saying, 'It's ok, really it's ok', but it didn't feel ok. Mum and I told the receptionist we had arrived. I heard her say to Mum, "I am sorry, but Dr B isn't here he has been called out on an emergency, but Dr Y will see you tonight, is this ok?"

"Yes," mum replied and we sat down and waited.

When my name was called, we walked into the doctor's room, sat there was a younger doctor, a foreign man. I think he was Swedish or something like that. He smiled at us and asked us to take a seat, he spoke directly to me, "I see Lynn, that the other doctor has booked you in for a termination," I nodded and started to cry. He sat forward on his chair, and smiled at my mum and me, then he said,

"You don't have to do this Lynn, you have other options." My eyes lit up. "You can keep this child if you want to – these choices cannot be made by others." My mum smiled, I thought she would be cross but I knew that she had also been dragged along with the idea of a termination, and was not quite so happy with this idea at all. So, it was settled, I was going to be a mum. I was ecstatic, unlike Mark's mum, who was really upset about the whole matter!

We were told we had to marry which we did on 14th February 1981. It felt very romantic, to marry the man you loved on St Valentine's Day. We would never forget that anniversary, I thought. The wedding was beautiful and Mark's grandmother made my dress; I was heavily pregnant at this time as the baby was due in March. They had postponed Mark's joining day for the navy until I had our baby. I went into hospital in heavy labour on 18th March 1981 - it was a terrifying time; I was just 2 months from my 17th birthday, but there were complications. I was terrified and after a few days in labour I was rushed to another hospital for an emergency caesarean. Eventually our beautiful daughter was born just after midnight on the 21st of March 1981, weighing in at 7lb 4oz.

We named her Nicola Diana. She was like a little doll; I loved her from the minute I met her. There was friction in Mark's family as his mum was angry that I had ruined her son's chances in life – everything had been delayed because of me. However, my voices told me this wasn't so and all would come right in the end. I didn't understand this until the country went to war and all those ships headed to the Falkland Islands. It was only then I grasped just what they had meant when they said he was being spared. The HMS Sheffield was one of the first ships to be blown out of the waters off the island; the chain of events that kept him at home had saved Mark's life.

We lived with my parents until Nicola was about two years old; we had been on the council waiting list for ages. I did love to still be at home, as Mum taught me all I needed to know about being a mum. I loved every minute of that time; it all came so naturally to me, being a mum was a huge part of my life's journey.

Mark moved in with us of course as we were now a married couple. The bond between grandparents and grandchild grew stronger and stronger. My dad couldn't bear to hear Nicky cry – he would sit for hours with her on his knee. "I have to say Dad, if you are watching me write these words over my shoulder, Nicky was spoilt rotten." How they loved her, she was the apple of their eye. When I look back, I couldn't have done all that in my young years without them both. They were an inspiration to me; I was a very lucky girl, I was blessed with the best parents a girl could ever wish for.

We had our names on the council waiting list for around 12 months but we were offered nothing in this time. This was ok with Mum and Dad as they loved to have us around the house. It was strange when I think back but I never heard my voices during this time and thank goodness the man at the top of the stairs seemed to have gone into hiding. He was a dark character and I do wonder now that I am surrounded with God's beautiful angels, had they come in and moved him on? That is something I will never know.

The day arrived when we received a letter telling us there was a house on a council estate in Noctorum. We jumped at it even though this estate was quite rough. We really wanted our own house and this was the only way to start. It was very challenging at first, as Nicky had been extremely spoilt living with her grandparents. I struggled to settle her during the day, she was very demanding and would never go to a nursery to meet other children; she just wanted to stay with me.

Mark and I would both work, he, during the day in an electrical wholesale warehouse and me, at night in nursing homes. That way we never had to ask for help with Nicky. We always knew that she was safe and sound with one of us. It was hard work being a young mum; I was only 19 when we moved into our first home, but this was my destiny in life, I know this for sure.

Mark and I were so very happy, he had a wonderful sense of humour; he used to make me laugh so much, we were perfect and in my eyes would live happily ever after. When Nicky was three and a half and soon to be starting school in the next September, I worried how she would be with this change in her life, as she didn't spend any time without us unless it was with her nanny and granddad. I would walk the five miles most afternoons to visit them in Moreton. I had a lovely, big old coach built pram, which made walking seem a dream. If nothing else it would always keep me fit and healthy, being on foot all the time.

It was in October 1984 I discovered I was expecting again; we were thrilled. I was just twenty years old. I loved my little family and I could see myself having lots of children, although I worried a little how I would cope as Nicky was constantly demanding. During this time, Mark had moved jobs; he picked up a job in Stevenage working with a big firm, and it was nearly double the money. The only downfall was that he would only be home at weekends. We missed him during the week but we managed.

Where we lived on the Noctorum, there used to be big marshlands. I had heard stories of people drowning many years ago in this place, and I felt they were just kidding me, trying to frighten me. It wasn't until I was around 7 months into my pregnancy that my contact with spirits started to happen again, the sightings of the man at the top of the stairs, and the strange noises in the house.

Nicky at this time had started pre-school which was fabulous as I managed to get some peace and quiet in the morning. It was one of those days when I didn't seem to get much done at all, and it was nearly time to go and pick Nicky up. I rushed to fetch her, feeling absolutely worn out. it was a Friday and Mark was due home that evening; he would get the train to the bottom of the estate and walk up.

After picking Nicky up from school, I asked her if she fancied a nap with mummy; we went upstairs and cuddled up. It wasn't long before we were both fast asleep when all of a sudden we heard a loud bang, it sounded like the front door. Nicky jumped up from her sleep and so did I, which at least made me feel that I wasn't imagining things! "It's daddy," she shouted, and we then heard someone come up the stairs and very strangely for Mark, go into Nicky's bedroom and shut the door.

We opened Nicky's bedroom door, which, I might add was open when we went for our nap, and there was no one there. "Where is Daddy?" Nicky asked. I just stood there in amazement at what had just happened. It was getting close to teatime now so both of us went downstairs and started to make tea. Mark arrived home around 5.30 and on telling him this story he told us we were both going daft, tickled Nicky and then it was all forgotten.

But was it?

The weeks went by until one July day I quite suddenly and unexpectedly went into labour with my baby. It was panic stations – my sister Cath and her boyfriend Paul were called and they came to look after Nicky. How exciting! Our new baby was on its way. Paul drove us to the hospital and Cath looked after Nicky. It was a quick labour – there was no time for pain relief. I remember saying this would be my last!

On the 23July 1985 weighing in at 7lb our beautiful son David was born. He was gorgeous; we were so blessed. He was so very different in temperament to Nicky as a baby and I believe this was because he hadn't lived with Nanny and Granddad. He was a pleasure, always smiling and happy and once he was able to, he would play for hours in his bedroom as a small child and was quite at home in his own company.

The house where we lived had a square landing at the top of the stairs, all the rooms led off it. Once David reached around four months old he went into his own room, which was to the left as you stepped off the stairs, and surrounded with toys, his cot always looked lost. The next room was ours, which was straight ahead in front of the stairs, and the room in the left-hand corner of the house was Nicky's. The family bathroom was also at the left of the stairs next to Nicky's room.

Mark had been made redundant from his job in Stevenage, which in one way was really a blessing as we now had a family and we needed Dad at home. He soon picked up some work and started a pools' round; sometimes this was hard for him as at that time of the year the nights where cold and dark. I so loved our life – it was just perfect in so many ways. We never had a lot of money but we were happy and that's all that mattered.

Mark was out one night doing his pools' round, when I was putting Nicky to bed. David was fast asleep already as he had gone to bed a little earlier. I had bathed Nicky and we were in my bedroom. The door was open and we could see the top of the stairs. I had Nicky wrapped in a towel on the bed trying to get her dry to put on her pyjamas.

We heard a noise on the landing, and both of us heard it. Nicky was only four at the time; we looked up and to my horror there was a man standing in the doorway of David's room. This was no living man! He was a very black shadow, tall but with no features that I could see. Nicky was terrified and I tried to stay calm but was also terrified. I told him to get out of my house and away from my children; he never spoke a word but turned and walked straight into David's room. I shot off my bed and ran in after him, except he was gone. I have to say I have never been so frightened. Had the man from our family home followed me? Who was this man? A million questions rolled around in my head. Mark was going to think I was out of my mind when he arrived home and I told him my account of events. I haven't thought about it until now as I am being reminded of these incidents, but this was to be the start of my daughter's 'knowing', or in other words, the beginning of her spiritual journey.

I saw this man several times over the coming months. He never spoke to me and always exited through David's bedroom. Luckily David would sleep through anything so this never disturbed him at all and he was oblivious to the whole thing. Nicky used to ask about 'the man at the top of the stairs', however, I used to make up a tale so that she wasn't frightened. I knew one thing for certain, I wasn't staying in that house much longer. We needed to find somewhere else to go – it wasn't a nice feeling seeing him near my children. Somehow, I always felt he couldn't harm us. I sensed a brighter energy close by when he came. I do believe now that this was my grandmother from across the park and she had come to protect us from this spirit.

As always, once I had taken Nicky into school I would walk to Moreton down a very long road, Manor Drive. On this day Mum and Dad were both at home, Dad had a swelling on his neck and it had grown quite big; when I arrived they told me that they were off to the doctors and that they would be home soon. They were gone such a long time and I had to be back to pick up Nicky from school, so I left them a note telling them I would see them soon and off I went on my long walk home.

Cath and Paul arrived the next day saying that they had a call from Mum and Dad wanting us to go to their house. They had something they wanted to talk to us about. I felt this dreadful feeling come over me. I didn't know why at the time, but now my guide Raoul tells me this was my guides drawing close to me, preparing me for bad news.

We arrived at Mum and Dad's, as always on opening the door I shouted, "is the kettle on?" and smiled. My dad was such a big tea lover his favourite saying was *put the kettle on make us a brew*. Mum stepped out from the kitchen and beckoned us in. There was Dad sitting at the kitchen table. "Sit down," Mum said. "There is a pot of tea on the table."

"What's going on?" we asked, "what's wrong?" I am sure that you all have had that feeling some time in your life when your stomach sinks, as you just know bad news is coming; well, this was one of those times.

Dad just sat there and didn't speak. Mum said, "Dad isn't too well. We have been to the hospital for some tests and the news is terrible. There is no easy way of saying this, Dad has cancer in his throat." I felt my heart sink.

"This can't be right,", we all said. "Are they sure?" This is our dad – this cannot be happening.

It was true and Dad was to start two years of gruelling chemotherapy and radiotherapy to save his life. It was around this time that they decided to move house into a smaller place, and Mum and Dad had made it possible for me and Mark to buy our family home, from them.

My sister Cath had decided that she would marry Paul and so they set out to arrange their wedding. This was 23 July 1988 my son's third birthday. It was a very emotional time, as Dad had undergone just over 16 months of treatment. We had wonderful news just before the wedding; the doctors had given Dad the all clear. We were all so happy our dad had come through and was going to be ok. The wedding was perfect and Dad looked so lovely in his top hat and tails; our family was safe.

Christmas that year was a huge family affair both – my sisters were expecting their first child and they were blooming. All was well with the world; what a lovely Christmas that was and I will never forget it as long as I live. We saw the New Year in with our lovely friends Aunty Doreen and Uncle Andrew. There was dancing and singing and Auld Lang Syne was sung in the street at full pelt, we were all so very happy. Dad was still very weak which I thought was from his chemotherapy but enjoyed the company; they left just after seeing in the New Year and went home to their little flat.

It was just weeks after all the celebration that the terrible news came. Mum told us that the dreaded cancer had reared its ugly head again. "He will be ok," she told us. "We will fight this together."

It was weird really because everything seemed calm; Mum and Dad were protecting us from what was going to happen. Dad had been told he was terminal and there was nothing they could do any more to help him. We were never told any of this. Mum and Dad carried this for months; they already knew before Christmas that Dad was poorly, but never told us so as to not ruin our Christmas.

I was working nights in Hoylake at the time; Mark was still doing his pools' round on the estate where we used to live. Things were hard because Dad wasn't very well again and he was a proud man and wouldn't let us girls do very much for him to help, which meant Mum carried her work and the heavy job of looking after a very ill man; I now know this was the cause of Mum's illnesses after my father passed.

I used to go straight to Clatterbridge Hospital to sit with Dad on the days he had to go there. He was always a joker. He would talk about the horses and life on Anglesey – always reminiscing. I didn't spend much time at home but I knew that my kids were ok with their dad.

It was one of my neighbours who brought something to my attention. "Lynn," she said, "I just can't watch this anymore. I know you have a lot on your plate with your dad being ill and you working nights but I need to tell you that there is a woman who comes at night while you are at work. She leaves in the morning around 6.30 before you are home."

I felt the bottom fall out of my world; I thought I had the perfect marriage. We loved each other so much and my kids adored their father. I confronted Mark, waiting for a logical explanation, but he just looked at me and told me that it was ok – this woman was his friend. He had met her on his pools' round last year; she had an open marriage and so should we!

My life flashed before me. I couldn't believe what I was hearing. "It's not all right with me!" I screamed at him. "I am so worried about my dad; how could you do this to me?"

I could hear my voices talking, *all will be well Lynn, all will be well.* I screamed at them also! "Go away," I said. "How could you let this happen to us?"

It was Sunday night and I had to go to work; I worked my night shift with all sorts running around my head. I received a call; it was Mum. "Come straight to the hospital Lynn, Dad is not good." My lovely friend gave me a lift that morning straight to the hospital. Dad was getting worse, his breathing was very bad. I had been with him the day before, and we had been chatting. Dad was distraught as this was the day of the Hillsborough disaster.

He was trying to talk to me, "What's going on?" he would say. He was very upset at what had happened; my dad loved his football and was a lifelong Liverpool fan.

When I arrived, they had moved Dad to his own room. He was hooked up to all sorts of monitors; the nurse had put up a drip for pain relief and Dad looked very frail. The doctor came in and told us that Dad was dying and we could stay with him as long as we wanted.

They were wonderful in that hospital. They looked after us so very well, we never left Dad's side. Dad's breathing was laboured and Mum and I sat either side of the bed holding one hand each. He only opened his eyes once during this time, and this was around 1a.m. on the Tuesday morning. He squeezed our hands, smiled and said, "Wow it's amazing." Then our dad shut his eyes and died that Tuesday morning 5 hours later, on the 18April 1989 at the age of 57.

Dad had seen heaven just before he passed; this made us feel a little better as we knew that Dad was home and pain-free and was reunited with his family who had passed before him.

There still are no words for the feelings that were running through my head that morning; everyone was called, and my sister Janet who lived in Stevenage, had a way to travel, heavily pregnant with her first child.

Cath's baby was due any day so Cath wasn't called – just my brother Steve; he picked up Mark from our house and headed to the hospital. I was in complete shock. I couldn't believe that my dad was gone; it was strange because something kept us calm: both Mum and I. We met with Steve and Mark in the waiting room of the hospital, then we all went back to the ward. The nurses had prepared Dad for us so we could say goodbye before we left.

We walked into the room and Dad lay in the bed where he died. I felt something in that room that day; I saw Dad standing over by the window. I saw him smile as his spirit left the room; it was peaceful as if I was floating somewhere else. I was angry with God for taking my dad; he was a good man with a big heart. Why would he take him; why not some person who was bad?

Hate is a very strong word and I now know that all these emotions were completely normal when you lose someone you love so dearly. I didn't hate God, but believe me I wasn't very happy with Him, and as far as I was concerned, I would never speak to him again. This was the end of all life as we knew it, our father was gone.

We left the hospital with the awful task of telling my sister what had happened. On heading to Steve's car, Mark told me that he had packed his things and was leaving me. Perfect timing. How cruel that was. For this, I would never forgive him.

We arrived at Cath's and as you can imagine, the news hit her like a ton of bricks. Dad's funeral was arranged quickly, as we had friends who owned Bell's Funeral Directors in Moreton. Cath had gone into labour on the morning of the 21April 1989. She watched as her dad's funeral cars passed the window of the hospital; this must have been terrible for her.

After the funeral, we held the wake at my house, our family home, and people came with us to toast our lovely dad. Then the telephone rang, it was Paul, my adorable nephew John had been born. Mum and baby were doing well. I do believe now that God had timed these things to help us with the loss of our father.

This has been a difficult chapter for me to write as I relive all those sad memories, but without it there would be a massive gap in the story, as indeed there was now a massive gap in my life. It has been 28 years now since my dad passed and the year is 2017. My dad is on my shoulder helping me to continue with this book. This brings great comfort to me, knowing he is still living his life with God and all his family who had gone before him. Dad and I have special signals for his presence and this always makes me giggle.

My father is with me and is guiding me through this book on a daily basis. I feel very blessed, and know my gift of medium-ship is God's way of repairing my past life, and the pain I felt at losing my dad.

My memories of my dad live on always loved, never forgotten. X

SIX

My Encounter with a Medium

It had been nearly two years since my lovely dad had passed and throughout that time, I had been so devastated at the loss of my father that I completely shut out God and my spirit team. I was only in my twenties and felt lost, devastated and angry with God; I didn't understand why he had done this to our family. I now know that this anger was grief and that I would soon learn to deal with my grief and be able to connect again.

As I have said in previous chapters of my book, Dad was an inspiration where God and spirit where concerned; he truly believed that when we passed we would move on to a beautiful stress-free place, this place being heaven. But nevertheless losing my dad knocked me for six; I wanted to believe that he was still around, and I was grief-stricken.

This was when I met my friend Barbara; I was living with my children Nicky and David in our old family home in Moreton. After Dad's passing, my mum had been taken quite ill; you see she had nursed my dad through two years of chemotherapy and quite frankly shear hell. This had taken its toll on my poor mum who wasn't much older than I am now. Mum's health started to go downhill quite dramatically over the coming years and my promise to my father would come into play before I knew it.

Over the year after my dad's passing, I would talk to God without listening for his answers. I would ask him why he had taken our dad? Why had he allowed my husband to leave us? Why was my mum suffering so? There were a lot of why's in those conversations with God and my spirit team, neither of whom could get through to me with the answers for which I was so desperately searching. You see, I just wasn't listening and consequently I felt that they had forsaken us.

It was close to the first anniversary of my father's passing when God used very clever tactics to make me listen again. I had been trying so hard to see my dad's face in my head and I was so worried about forgetting what he looked like. I would talk to him when lying in the dark of the night, and not being able to sleep. It was around four in the morning and I awoke after a lovely dream. I had dreamt that my dad was standing in the kitchen of our family home; he stood just out of reach of me, in fact, he was stood by the door to the back garden. He would chat to me and tell me everything was ok, he told me that he was pain-free and that heaven was everything and more.

I awoke with a bit of a shock thinking that Dad was actually there with me. But the strangest thing happened: every time I fell back to sleep, we were right back in the kitchen and I had the kettle on making tea and Dad was chatting to me from the corner of the kitchen. This happened for a whole week, night after night; it was so comforting to speak with Dad telling him about all that had happened since he passed.

I felt awake again as if new life had been breathed into me. God had used my dreams to show me my dad; he had brought him home to me and allowed Dad to chat with me a while. The last dream I had that week was Dad telling me just before he left that God had plans for me, and I was to listen to my guides again, as God was talking and he would use these guides and the angels to teach me what I needed to know to move on with my life.

It was some months later that a friend who lived a few doors down told me she was going to see a medium in Moreton. She asked would I go with her; I had never been to see a medium before so I was a little apprehensive, but I agreed to go with her. It was an afternoon appointment and the sun was shining and it was indeed a beautiful day. We strolled through the park to a road quite close by; we knocked on the door of this little bungalow only five minutes' walk from our house then the door opened and there stood a man. He asked us in and showed us to the front living room. He invited us to take a seat and informed us that Barbara would be with us shortly.

This was the first time I met my lovely friend Barbara; little did I know that there would be a special connection with us for many years to come and many more beautiful stories for me to tell you. The door opened and in walked a little lady whom I can only describe as a little welsh doll. She had the most beautiful clear blue eyes and those eyes seemed to see right through into your soul.

"Hello," she said, "who is first?" I spoke up and told her I was only here to keep my friend company, as she didn't want to come alone – I hadn't come for a reading. She looked straight at me and said, "You are first, Lynn." I shook my head feeling quite anxious, to be honest. "I have things to say to you Lynn," she continued.

My friend stared at me and said, "Go on Lynn, you first." I felt a warm feeling come over me as if I knew everything would be ok, so I stood up and followed Barbara into another room.

I sat down not knowing what to expect, she asked me to shuffle a pack of playing cards. I did so, then placed them down on the little table in front of me. Barbara started to cough, clearing her throat as she was trying to talk to me. "I am sorry," she said, "but I feel a spirit close to us; I feel this man has passed with something to do with his throat, as he is clearing his throat and coughing as I listen to him. He is dressed head to toe in a blue uniform of some kind, I cannot make out if it is RAF or police," she continued.

I stared at her with my mouth open! She was talking to my dad, he always showed himself in the RAF uniform so I would know it was him. "He has a lot to tell you Lynn, he tells me he has been communicating with you in your dreams; he wants you to know that he is ok – all is well now. He has no pain anymore and he is at peace in heaven. Life will become better for you Lynn as I know you are finding it very hard at the moment," my lovely dad told me through Barbara. "You will meet someone who will sweep you off your feet, and you will be head over heels in love with this man. Enjoy your life Lynn and remember I am always close by, just think of me and I will be there."

"There will be more children, I feel two," she said.

"Oh, good Lord," I quietly thought to myself.

"You will have a full life Lynn, but remember you have been put here with a task to do; you are here to help people as I do."

In my mind, I was thinking, 'this lady is nuts, I can barely help myself; I am a single mum with two young children'.

It was as if she read my mind as she then told me that I would spend my life in aid of others. All my jobs would be caring for someone, spreading my love to others. At this time, I worked in home care with social services; it was indeed a job I loved. Seeing those faces of the elderly as I walked in to help with breakfast, giving those hugs to those who don't see anyone from day to day, I really did love my job.

I just stared at this lady in amazement. "You don't believe me Lynn, do you? He has asked me to tell you about your dreams; he has been to you several times in your family home. He is very close by and is watching over you and the children from heaven." I was amazed that she knew these things, how was it possible?

I left her house that day a changed woman; I knew my father was around us and that he was at peace in heaven. This brought me a comfort I struggle to explain, but it does come flooding back to me every time someone comes here for a reading. The tears are usually flowing with my clients; they always tell me that I have brought them an understanding, I had brought them some peace of mind. Little did I know on that day when I met Barbara, that this was also to be my journey but not until many years later.

It was as if Barbara had flicked on a switch in me; I started to hear the voices of my guides again in my head. I felt they started to structure what was to be my new life, although they didn't speak to me often, I knew they were present in most of my decisions.

Life moved on quite quickly. I felt different somehow, my awareness of spirit had come back and I felt so much lighter. It's one thing having that awareness but another actually knowing what was being said to me. I struggled with making my mind quiet, after all I was only a young woman still in my early twenties, with two young children, so there was nothing quiet in my life too often. I know now that spirits kept very quiet during these times in my life. They wanted me to heal and to enjoy all that was happening to my family and me.

It was only months after going for that reading that I met a man who was to become my husband; it was quite funny really because this man had lived three doors down all of my life.

He was a quiet man but always gave me a warming glance as I walked by; his name was Ken and was the brother-in-law of my friend whom I had accompanied to the reading that day with Barbara. June told me how Ken fancied me; I was quite shy and blushed at the thought of anyone other than my husband who had left us. It had been nearly two years now since my husband had left and I had plodded on with my life thinking I was fine with how life was and how I wouldn't trust anyone ever again. This had been all too painful, and I had to put on my invisible armour, to protect me from someone ever hurting us again. We divorced quickly, as he had met another lady. I had zero help from him and he pushed his two beautiful children out of his life.

His two children are now 36 and 32 with children of their own; he has missed out on the most wonderful moments of our children's lives, but you see I recall something a friend said to me once which I thought was a bit close to the bone. "Any man can father a child, but it takes a great man to actually be a good father." Well, there was never a truer word said. Being both Mum and Dad had been a tough journey for me, but I survived and so did my kids. My life has been devoted to them and will be until the day I die. My journey with my children and grandchildren is for life, till death do us part, and I will always uphold those vows to my wonderful children.

After a few weeks, June asked if I would like to go out to the pub with her, she said there was a band on in Moreton and it would be fun. It wasn't until that night she arrived at my front door to collect me she said, "Oh yes, I forgot to say my hubby and his brother are coming too." I looked at her and she smiled.

"You planned this, didn't you," I asked laughing.

"Who, me?" she replied.

I felt alive again as Dad said I would. Ken was a true gentleman, unlike many men these days. He would open the door for me, and never let me go to the bar to buy a drink; he treated me like a true princess. After many months of dating, it became obvious to everyone that we were both head over heels in love with each other. He was good to my two children Nicky and David, and helped with things they needed and he bought Nicky her first horse, which really was beyond what was expected of him.

He was a funny character, really very quiet, except with me. I think people thought he had attitude, at least until they got to know him. But to me he was always wonderful, very much the romantic. He would spoil me rotten, and when he did, he would do it with such love.

I would catch him staring at me sometimes and when I did he would smile and tell me how lucky he was to have found me; I had never been so happy. I make him sound like a Saint, don't I? But no one is without flaws. Unfortunately, Ken was a drinker. He worked very hard at his job but in the evening, he would drink; in my opinion, far too much. One thing I will say is that he was never violent. He was one of those drinkers who would just fall over and go to sleep. I loved him so much that I overlooked what he was doing every night and loved him for all the good things he did and not the one thing that was wrong. But in my gut, I knew this was not going to turn out well.

It was around two years into our relationship that I found out I was pregnant with my youngest son Chris. I was thrilled. I always wanted lots of children; Ken however, was a little shocked. He didn't want any more children, as he had two daughters who he didn't see. I didn't know why at the time, until our son Chris started suffering with anxiety and panic attacks. Ken was worried that if he had children, they would turn out like him. You see, I now know that Ken drank to make him feel better. He would also feel anxious and didn't like being around too many people. It was many years before I found out about this similarity and realising this was also Ken's problem. It made so many pieces of the jigsaw fit into place.

The lane where we lived (which is the same place that I live now, just different ends of the lane) is cut in half by the railway line but this lane stretches all the way to the beach where I walked as a young child with my sister. We lived at this time near the park and the school; there were people in this road who were not very nice and quite frankly drove most of us around the bend with their ways. As I said earlier, I lived in the home where I had grown up as child. I loved our family home but it was time for Ken and I to make a new start, in a home of our own but if it hadn't have been for Mum and Dad's kindness, I would never have been able to buy my first home, or indeed move on in my life at the time.

They sold it to us for a very low price, just enough for them to be able to buy their little flat. They helped with everything: the solicitor's fees and moving costs. In those days, you could get a 100% mortgage, as the government was trying to encourage people to buy rather than rent.

On making the decision that I would sell my home and make a new life with Ken somewhere else, we set out looking for something we both liked. We looked everywhere. Ken had a good job and I still worked in nursing homes, so I knew we would be able to get a mortgage very easily. I could hear the spirits' encouragement all through the process of moving. I was now around five months into my pregnancy, all was going well, we had a letter through the front door telling us there was a housing association buying properties in our area and they were interested in our house. We snapped up their offer, as we hadn't had many people around to look. They had offered us nearly three times what I had paid when I bought it from Mum and Dad.

The only problem was that we had to be out in 4 weeks! I was heavily pregnant and we had nowhere to go! It was very stressful, things moved very fast. I looked and looked for a new house and found one in Wallasey that we loved. Unfortunately, the people couldn't move into their new home for weeks, so we had to find a stop-gap of many weeks. Ken's mum offered us her home, which was so very kind of her, as I had two young children also.

It wasn't until I was nearly eight months pregnant that we actually moved into our new home in Wallasey. This was a really stressful pregnancy! I was exhausted, but in my mind I knew it would all be ok. We moved into this new home in May 1993 and on the 10th July 1993 our beautiful son Chris was born. Our life was perfect, I was so very happy I had a man who loved me like no other could and I had three beautiful children and our own home. I felt so complete, except for one thing, I wanted to be married to the man I loved so dearly.

I felt that the spirits had been very quiet during the past years since I met Barbara. I think during this part of my life I had to find myself and learn to love again and be happy. Everything that Barbara had told me in my reading had come true, I couldn't believe my luck and I was so very happy. Ken and I decided to marry and I started to plan our wedding; I was lucky to have my younger sister Cath who was absolutely fantastic at organizing a party. So, I asked her to help me which now, looking back on the circumstances which unfolded, I could never have done without. My big sister Jan also helped and I realised after this story unfolded, that none of it would have happened without Cath's skills and hard work. We set to work planning and the church was booked for 24th September 1994. I was so excited, Ken however, was less excited as he hated any attention being on him but he wanted me to be happy so he just went with the flow, as I think most men do really.

We had booked the venue and all was going well. I had given Cath a budget to work to, this was for the food and other things. Then something happened; it was about 10 days before the wedding. I had experienced some pain in my lower abdomen. I wasn't one of these people who moaned about pain, I just got on with it. I had been diagnosed many years earlier with a condition called endometriosis. This caused me a lot of pain and it wasn't getting any better. I would suffer quite a lot of pain from this condition so most of the time I would put everything down to that illness.

It was a school morning and my son David was ready to go to school. I would walk him to school, as he was only 8 years old. I was in the bathroom and collapsed. Christopher was downstairs in his highchair as he was only 14 months old. David heard the thud as I collapsed in the bathroom. Ken had already gone to work around 6.30. David and Nicky ran up the stairs to see what had happened and there I was in a heap on the bathroom floor. Nicky watched Chris while David ran around the corner to my friend's and told her to come quickly. On arrival I told Karen what had happened. She told me to call the doctor's straight away and that she would put Chris in his pram and take the children to school for me. I had known Karen since I was just 12 years old. We met in school and she has become a lifelong friend, whom I love dearly.

I could hear a voice as clear as day saying, 'hurry Lynn, your life is in danger'. I called the doctor's straight away. He told me to come straight to the surgery; I felt awful but walked down to the doctor's surgery which was very close to my home. On examination, he said that I was very ill and I had an ectopic pregnancy. I was shocked, as I didn't know much about this condition. "Your life is in danger, Lynn," he said, "I must call an ambulance straight away." There were no such thing as mobile phones in those days so I couldn't tell Karen and she had my son with her at the school.

I told the doctor I had to wait. Before I left the doctor's, Karen had arrived. She said she had knocked on my door and saw the note I had left to say where I was. The doctor called the ambulance and I was taken straight to the hospital. Karen took Chris home and kept him until my mum could get there on the bus from Moreton. Ken knew nothing of all this until he arrived home at 6pm that evening. I was so frightened and just wished that Ken was with me but it's a good job he wasn't as what happened next, I do feel he might have throttled the doctor!

The doctor arrived to examine me. He was arrogant and rude. If it had been today, I would have given him a piece of my mind, but I was only young – still in my twenties. He told me that I was having a miscarriage. By now I was screaming with the pain. He was a horrible man! He shouted at me and said, "You have had three children, woman, get a grip; this pain is not as bad!"

I had to disagree. I was in absolute agony; he decided that he would take me down to theatre and do a procedure called a D&C. This would clear away all that was left and the pain would go away.

This doctor performed the surgery and as with all surgery, anything that is removed is taken to the lab for inspection. I was discharged from the hospital and sent home and told to get a grip and take paracetamol.

My voices where telling me I was in danger, the doctor was telling me to get a grip and don't be so childish, I didn't know where I was. I felt so ill but went home to bed. The very next day I had a phone call from the doctor's surgery and I was to go to hospital straight away and they were sending an ambulance to take me. They had found nothing in my D&C, which meant the pregnancy was somewhere else, and my doctor was right all along, I had an ectopic pregnancy and it was now at a critical stage and I was in danger of losing my life.

It was like emergency ward 10! I was rushed by blue light to the hospital and was greeted by a young Australian lady doctor. She told me that she was so very sorry and that there had been a mistake. I was taken to theatre within minutes of my arrival absolutely screaming with the intense pain. When I woke up, Ken was at my side; he was so distraught as the surgery had been performed just in time to save my life.

It's funny but although all this was going on around me I knew I wasn't in any danger as my voices had told me it would be ok. I thought I was hearing things, but they were as clear as day in my head. 'You are fine Lynn', they would say. 'You will live'. The doctor came and spoke with us, telling us that I had indeed had an ectopic and that the baby was nearly 12 weeks but could not be saved. She told me she didn't know how I had got to 12 weeks as usually the pain from conception with an ectopic is intense. All I knew was that I was safe and this doctor had saved my life. Things certainly could have turned out very differently but it wasn't my time.

Needless to say, I never heard of that arrogant male doctor again; my children could have lost their mother because of his negligence. When I look back now I really should have pursued this with the courts and this man should have been struck off as a gynaecologist, but I was grateful to be alive, so I took this no further.

There was a little matter of my wedding. This all happened around 10 days before our wedding day. The vicar from the church came to visit me in hospital. "Lynn," he said, "you don't realise what you have been through. This has been a matter of life and death. We should postpone the wedding and move it to another date, you are so very weak and it is only 4 days until the big day."

"I am fine," I said to him. I could hear my voices very strongly, 'All will be well Lynn', they would say.

"I don't want to cancel, I will be married on Saturday."

"We will see," he told me and he blessed me and left. Ken was smiling at me from across the room.

"You are so stubborn," he said to me. I smiled and told him, "Hey it's taken years to get you to marry me; I am not giving up now." Ken just laughed kissed me and told me he would see me later today.

Lying in that hospital bed I could hear the spirit so

clearly. 'You are in a lot of pain', they said to me. 'You must rest'. It was Tuesday evening and I can't tell you how much pain I was in, because of the mess the ectopic had made inside me. The scar was very big, almost 16 inches long! I felt like I had been sawn in half! The pain was intense. I spoke to the voices in my head, sometimes out loud; the nurses told the doctor that I was hallucinating. Of course I wasn't. The spirits had stepped in to help me to settle. I wasn't going to let this stand in the way of my wedding. My sister Cath had completely taken over the planning and I do believe had well gone over my budget by now, as she prepared a wedding fit for a princess! For this Cath, I will always remember and love you dearly.

It was now Thursday morning, the doctors had come to assess me, and they said I was making good progress. They all knew in the hospital that my wedding was set for Saturday; they didn't however, know how I was planning to make it to the church. Nothing was keeping me from my wedding day and so I told them that I was going home. The doctors were not happy with this idea. "You don't know what you are asking of yourself Lynn," they told me. "You have been through a terrible ordeal and are lucky to be alive."

"I have heard that too many times this week," I told them. "I AM alive and I will be at my wedding."

"I wouldn't argue with her," Ken told the doctors, "when she sets her mind to something, there is no stopping her," he laughed.

I discharged myself from hospital that afternoon and went home; I was in so much pain but battled on regardless. It was the night of my rehearsal and I could hardly walk. My sister Jan told me that she would go to the church and stand in for me. I imagine Ken was not too happy about that. I can see his face now, frowning at the idea of greeting my big sister at the bottom of the aisle. This truly makes me giggle as I write these words today.

I had gone to bed early crying with the pain in my stomach. I remember taking some very strong painkillers and hoping all would just be ok in the morning. It wasn't ok, in fact it was far from ok. I was in a really bad way. My doctor came to visit and told me the painkillers were effecting my stomach, and this was causing more pain and pressure. He gave me something to help me to sleep as tomorrow was the big day. My poor mum had been run ragged as she was looking after the kids while Ken was at work, everything was a disaster! I felt very emotional.

I cried and cried and was begging for help. "Where are you, Dad, are you there?" I cried. "You told me that you would come if I called, I need your help. I am in so much pain, and it's my wedding day tomorrow." I must have cried myself to sleep that Friday night, as I awoke to the sun shining through my window and the birds singing on that special September morning. It was around 11am I heard a tap on the door. It was Jan. "And, how are you feeling?" she asked. I was frightened to answer as I actually felt ok. "I have brought you a cup of tea, sit there and drink it – don't jump up out of bed."

I sat up in bed with my cuppa and enjoyed the sunshine streaming through the window. I felt calm and relaxed and surprisingly very little pain. I swung my legs out of bed and reluctantly stood up. I made my way downstairs; everyone was in the kitchen, which is where the women of this family seem to gather. Ken had stayed at his mum's so not to see the bride and to everyone's amazement I walked in as if there was nothing wrong. I felt very little pain, and actually felt on cloud nine.

No one could believe it; this was a miracle. I had gone from one extreme to the other, from not being able to walk, to feeling wonderful. Mum told me to take it easy for the next couple of hours or things could change dramatically. The photographer arrived to film the time before the wedding. Then the time came to go to the church. A family friend Sue, who I had spoken about in my very early chapters, had married a man who owned a wedding and funeral business in Moreton. She had given the use of a silver ghost Rolls Royce as a gift for our wedding day. The car arrived to take my mum and my children to the church, and I was sat quietly with my brother Steve who was giving me away in place of our lovely dad. I was quietly nervous but felt a lot of comfort from somewhere. There was still not much pain, just a little twinge. I arrived at the church and the organ began to play the wedding march. My brother had hold of my hand tightly. "You will be ok," he assured me. "Just take it easy – there is no rush."

At the moment he said those words, I felt a rush all over my body. I felt someone take my other arm, my brother to my right and someone else took my arm to my left. I was lifted as if I was floating, I moved down the aisle with great ease. The wedding was perfect and my father had heard my cries. He had come to help me in my desperate state. In my brother's speech he said, "I was worried how Lynn would cope with that walk down the aisle but to my surprise she seemed to float as if she was on rollerskates."

I felt my father beside me; I know he heard the spirits and they guided him to his daughter on her special day. The pain however had not gone, God had given me time out. It was just after the wedding reception that the pain came straight back, not quite as bad but there nevertheless. I thank God for hearing my prayers. I feel blessed by the miracle he bestowed on me that very special day.

All that Barbara had told me was right, I had never been so happy and God and the angels took a big part in making that day perfect for me and Ken. But this wasn't the last time I would call on God so dramatically and to this day he never lets me down.

For these blessings, I am truly grateful.

SEVEN

Our Return to Home Ground

We had lived quite happily in Wallasey for many years. Ken was still working hard as a joiner and I was working in a daycare for mentally ill people, mostly Alzheimer's and dementia patients. I loved my job but I felt my roots calling me. We decided to put our house up for sale and move back to where we both had come from originally.

We sold quite quickly and we bought a lovely house in Moreton only a stone's throw from where we had both grown up. It had a lovely garden and the house was detached. How I loved this house; it was here that my mum would come to live with us for the first time.

She had been quite ill living in that flat in Upton and so she moved out into sheltered accommodation. She was very immobile at the time as her hips had broken down quite badly; her heart was also failing so there was nothing else to do. We needed to bring her into our home and care for her properly. Mum and

Ken got on so well and he adored her. She always had so much time for him and would listen to his tales of his family and his work on a daily basis.

It was around 18 months after moving into our new home that Ken decided he would convert the garage into a bedroom for Mum. He had finished the foundations and put in the floor when Mum decided that she couldn't possibly move in, as there was no downstairs bathroom only a toilet. Kenny was good at building but not very experienced at plumbing and to convert the downstairs to a wet room would take some considerable work. He had got as far as putting in the roof when he had an accident while he was fishing on Anglesey.

I couldn't believe it when he walked through the door. He had ridden his motorbike over a hundred miles in complete agony. He had fallen down a crevice in the rock face and smashed his elbow joint and his upper arm. He was a mess; he was lucky to be alive.

Ken ended up in surgery and his arm was pinned and plated but was never as strong as it used to be. However, he insisted in pushing on with the room for Mum, sometimes working with one arm. There was no talking to him when he set his mind to something; he was going to do it. Even though Mum said she couldn't come, my voices where telling us to finish as she would change her mind. We thought we might as well finish what had been started and make the garage into a room anyway and then when she changed her mind it would be ready for her to move into.

It was while this room was being done that Dad made a visit to my son David. David was around 17 years old now and was sleeping in the room while it was being finished. When Mum said she didn't want it as it would be too much trouble, we told David that he could have the room.

One night he was with his girlfriend. They were both fast asleep and to his girlfriend's horror, she heard a voice saying, 'David wake up'. She was frozen to the bed and didn't want to look, as this was a voice she didn't recognise and she said that she felt the bed sink as if someone had sat next to them. Then came the voice trying to wake David up.

David sat bolt upright in bed and spoke with this person. This man's voice said, 'Thank you, David for giving your bedroom to Nan, as she is frail and unwell. She is very unhappy and her mood is very low. You are a good boy and Nan will be safe now here with her family'. Then David fell back to sleep and needless to say remembered very little in the morning. His girlfriend was terrified and didn't stay much after that. It seemed to ease her when we told her who it was, and that Granddad had come to say to David, well done and thank you.

On careful thought Ken and I decided we would use our savings for the downstairs toilet to be converted into a wet room. We called a bathroom shop and they arranged the whole thing. It didn't take too long and before we knew it, Mum had changed her mind as the angels had told me and moved in with us. It was a relief, I must say as she was beginning to be quite depressed and my siblings and I were worried about her being alone.

It was around 2002 now and this was the year that my marriage took a turn for the worse. This around 2 years after Mum had moved in with us. Ken and I couldn't agree upon the worry I had over the excess drinking. My life fell to pieces the day we split up, as we loved each other so much. I wish now, looking back, that I had looked into the why...why he drank, what was he drowning with this habit? These answers of course I now have. Like his son, he too suffered with anxiety and the drink numbed the feeling for him. I truly felt if we split for a while that all would be fixed, as we couldn't bear to be apart from each other, so I helped Ken to move into a house not far from us and hoped he would have some time to reflect. The wedge between us got bigger and bigger and the marriage was never reconciled. For this, I am truly sorry. There are not many loves like ours in one lifetime and with both our stubborn ways, we would never be a couple again.

It was now around 5 years on and this was the year that I met Ray my current husband. To say Ray and I met each other by accident is very true; both of us were lonely and looking for someone to share our lives with and by some twist of fate we found each other. Ray is a very quiet, unassuming man and I have to say can come across as quite rude sometimes, as he isn't good around people he doesn't know either. Looking back now, I see a pattern forming here! Ray soon became a part of our family and my children, who were now adults, just loved him to bits and although Ray is not the grandchildren's biological grandfather, there is no better granddad in this world for them, he loves them so much and is fantastic with them.

These times were never easy as Mum was quite ill now, although only young still, she was in heart failure and her hip had broken down with arthritis. She was on a hospital waiting list for a hip replacement. The day came after lots of care at home, when Mum received her appointment from the hospital. We were all very anxious about this as they told us that Mum was very high risk of dying under the anaesthetic, with having a bad heart and breathing problems.

Mum's quality of life was not high, she spent a lot of time sitting in her chair doing nothing. Mum was around the age of 70, which these days is not old by any stretch of the imagination. Mum went into the hospital and came through the surgery with flying colours; she started to walk within hours of it being done. It was a fabulous sight; she was thrilled and was told she could come home into my care.

Within 48 hours of being home, she started to act quite strangely. Her memory started to worsen and things were not good. She started to vomit and her hip was very swollen. We sent for the doctor straight away. He came very quickly and told us Mum had an infection in her hip joint. She was taken by ambulance to the nearest hospital and taken to A&E and on examination they saw a very small mark on her scar; they got a swab and started to examine it. They touched it with the swab and the worst thing happened, the hip burst out like a bursting dam. There was around a litre or more of infection all over the floor, her swab was taken to the lab and that is when we received the terrible news, our mum had caught CDIFF, the hospital bug!

Mum was extremely ill now and her body wasn't reacting to the antibiotics. She was dying slowly before our eyes. The bug had eaten away her bowel and they called us in and told us they would have to operate. Mum was desperately ill and had to have part of her bowl removed immediately or she would not survive.

The surgery went well but Mum came out with a colostomy bag. They told us it wasn't permanent and that she could have it reversed in around 2 years if all went to plan. Mum wasn't out of the woods yet though, she was still desperately ill. As a family, we took turns morning, noon and night to go into the hospital to help to feed her. The staff were wonderful but there just weren't enough of them to help with Mum's care, and this went on for 6 months.

It was my turn to do the lunch time visit; I turned up to a very weak mum. She hadn't done a lot of talking over the 6 months; she was often oblivious to us being there, but on this day she looked at me as I came on the ward. "I can't do this anymore Lynn," she said. Now if you knew my mother, you would realise those words coming from her were not good. She is a fighter and nothing ever beats her. I asked her what did she mean? "You're going to be ok, you have come through the worst."

"I can't go on," she said. "I just want to die now. I am not staying here." The look on her face told me that she was deadly serious.

"I am going to let go," she told me.

"You are not," I replied. "You have too much to live for, Mum." I could feel the tears building up inside me. "You must fight, you haven't seen your great grandson for 7 months and he misses you." My grandson Joe was only 3 years old at the time and was mum's first great grandchild. She adored him and vice versa but because of mum's illness they wouldn't allow him into the hospital. I was not going to sit back and watch my mother slip away; I made my excuses and went to the nurse's station. I told the nurse what Mum had said and told her that the only thing that would make her fight was a visit from Joe.

As Mum was on an open ward, not a side ward, I didn't see the problem. Visitors were in and out daily with Mum being on the same ward as their relatives, without anyone turning a hair. I made a phone call to my daughter Nicky and told her to get in a taxi and bring Joe with her, as Nan was giving up and this was not happening on my watch!

Within the hour, Nicky arrived. I hadn't told Mum of my plans; I took Joe by the hand and walked him into the ward. Stood at the side of Mum's bed, I announced to her that she had a visitor. She was curled up like a little old woman in her bed, not much life in her. She had already started to give up. Mum turned to see who had come to visit; it was remarkable what happened next. She pushed herself up in her bed, and a beaming smile came over her face.

"Oh, my lovely boy," she said with tears in her eyes, "you have come to visit me." Joe was thrilled to see his little nanny and he had missed her so much.

Mum introduced Joe to the other ladies in the ward. She very proudly told them that this was her first great grandson. She told them how clever he was and that she loved her time with him; the sight of my lovely grandson had breathed new life into our mum. Joe entertained the whole ward for 40 minutes. Everyone loved this little blond-haired boy. He had given life to those very poorly people that day, and a smile all over those faces that earlier had looked gloomy and sad. They had all received love and healing from a tiny child.

I knew Mum wasn't free from this debilitating illness yet and my brother and sisters and I continued to visit different times so that she had someone with her all day.

My voices were talking to me at what felt like 100 miles an hour. I didn't understand much of it but I just knew there was something that they could do to help us. So, I set to work. I decided to call everyone I knew and ask them would they join us in a powerful prayer hour. I wrote out a prayer asking God and the angels to heal our mum. I made a lot of phone calls to over 80 people. I asked that they help and all said yes. I asked for them to say the prayer at the same time every night for a few days, 8 pm to be exact. They all agreed to do this for our lovely mum, as most of them had known her all of their lives.

Whist making these calls I came across a few people who had completed their Reiki Healing courses; these friends told me they would also send distance Reiki to Mum at 8 pm every night.

I felt confident that we had such a force behind us now, and God would hear our prayers.

Mum was one of life's miracles; within 6 weeks of the prayer group praying every night she had made enough of a recovery that they allowed our mum to come home.

God had stepped forward and helped Mum back to her feet and as for the Reiki healing that was sent to our mum, this was my first introduction to Reiki, and it wouldn't be my last. The power of the prayer and the healing from spirits, had delivered Mum home to us at last.

Mum arrived home fighting fit and I just knew all would be well. During our time in the Moreton house some strange things would happen. I remember one evening it was around 8 pm. My mum shouted me and told me to get Christopher in out of the garden. I looked at her, "Mum," I said, "he is in bed and has been for an hour." My mum pointed to the back garden. We could hear the toys playing music and there to my surprise was a little boy, with blond hair and he was sitting on our lawn playing with the toys which had been left out from Joe's visit earlier that day. Mum looked at me and we both realised that it was the spirit of a child, whom we had never seen before. He looked up at us and smiled. Sadly, we never saw him again but many a night while lying in my bed I would hear the sound of the musical toys playing in the garden shed. My guides now tell me that the little boy was lost but he has now found his way into the light and is safely at home with his family.

The voices of the angels never let me forget the healing which Mum had received at that time; they told me that healing was to be part of my future, but not quite yet.

EIGHT

The Lifelong Dream

Mum had been out of hospital a good while now; she wasn't the same woman anymore, in fact she was quite weak. At this time in my life I was doing well with my new career. I had left the care home world and met a man who had told me he would teach me sales, and so for years now, I had been selling holiday homes and villas on the beautiful island of Cyprus. Even though I would have loved a property myself on the island, my heart still remained in the UK.

Ray and I had seen a property in the local newspaper, a stunning 17 century farmhouse in Holywell, North Wales; it had been dramatically reduced in price, whic was, I thought, a sign for me to jump right in and buy it. The property was the most stunning place you had ever seen. When you drew up to the property it had the most commanding large black and gold electric gates, which led to a long driveway sloping down into a small valley. At the bottom of the driveway, to the left, was a very large stable block with seven stables and a large hay barn. The property had four acres of fields which was just enough for my horses. At the time, I had Serene my mare that I have now had for 21 years. I had another called Amy who was a troubled soul and wasn't doing very well with her owners so I bought her and I had a little Shetland pony called Bill, we also had a full breed shire horse who I had bought for Ray as a gift so that we could go for rides on Halkyn Mountain together. Jake his name was; he was a very big horse and at times could be quite the handful. As you pulled around a small roundabout at the bottom of the driveway, there stood the most beautiful grey Welsh stone house. The house was very large and mainly on one floor and at one end of the house was four good-sized rooms. I decided we would make this into a granny flat for Mum, so Ray and his uncle set to work to put in a small kitchen and bathroom-come-wet-room. It didn't take long before it was finished and we could all move in to our new home. We moved in to the new house in November 2006; we were all so very excited – a new start in Wales, a place which both of us had loved most of our lives.

We were only two minutes from the A55 road which took us quickly straight back to Wirral as Chris was still attending his school there. Also, David and Nicky were still living in their own places on the Wirral so I was happy not having too far to commute to see them.

It took us a while to unpack and settle in but we were so happy, or so we thought. Mum absolutely loved her little granny flat and she looked out over butterfly gardens full of apple trees and beautiful shrubs. I felt we could be happy here, I really did. We had a Christmas get together and invited both sides of the family. My kids stayed over and Christmas was just perfect.

January to me always seems a gloomy month and this one of 2007 was no different to any other. Christmas had come and gone and we were all looking forward to Spring. Where our house was situated presented the most breath-taking views across the River Dee. On a clear day, we could see the whole of the Wirral coastline from the famous ice cream shop in Parkgate, up to the tip of West Kirby. The view was amazing and in the evening the whole coastline seemed to light up with twinkling fairy lights. We were in heaven that was for sure, or was this just a trick of my imagination?

We were all pretty fed-up with winter and were looking forward to our first Spring and Summer here in our new home. My kids had come to stay over for the weekend with their partners; we had a few drinks and a lovely meal. Because we had converted most of the downstairs for Mum, there were only three bedrooms upstairs, for us to use and our daily living space down stairs, which was a little cramped when the whole family came to visit, but we managed.

Nicky had to sleep downstairs on one of the couches. On one occasion we were awoken to Nicky screaming which believe me, didn't go down well with her nan! We went down and all she kept saying was, "There is a ghost, there is a ghost!" Now if she hadn't shown me the evidence, I would have thought that one too many drinks had been consumed the night before.

Nicky had used her phone and recorded the paranormal activity; she was terrified, she told me that she couldn't get off the couch as every time she moved the thing she could see would get faster and faster! I viewed the footage and to my surprise there it was, the orbs were huge, they were bouncing off the walls, great big blue orbs. I didn't feel anything bad about this phenomenon – I felt quite protected but I understood why Nicky was panicking as it certainly was a sight to see. These very visible energies where friendly and meant us no harm and it wasn't the last time they would come and in such numbers.

In the evening, the house had a very eerie feel. Chris grew more and more isolated and Ray and I had more and more arguments. All in all, we were not enjoying the house at all. One night we had lit the log burner in the main living room. I couldn't get warm no matter what we did, then all of a sudden, the fire turned a burning orange. It glowed as if we had thrown fuel onto the burning wood.

Then she appeared! The face of an old-fashioned lady. She looked very stern with her hair dragged back from her face in a topknot and very dark black eyebrows. She was quite a scary sight; her face was in the glass on the fire front. I had a feeling of dread come over me, as she appeared, then quite quickly disappeared. I did take some photographs but they didn't do that scene any justice to be honest, it just looked like a smudge on the glass. I wasn't the only person to see this face. My son Chris and Ray were in the room with me at the time. That was the only time we saw her face but we all felt a presence within the room and upstairs in the main bit of the house.

It was now summer on our lovely mountain; Halkyn Mountain was such a peaceful place and full of ancient wisdom. We had spent a hard winter in our new home and we all felt very grumpy and in need of some summer sunshine, or so we thought. It had been a bad winter and at one point we were snowed in, because the driveway was so steep, when the snow fell we just couldn't get any vehicle up to the main road. There were a lot of arguments over that winter, mostly to the tune of, 'we should never have moved here'!

We had seen the orbs quite a lot over the winter months usually when we had felt the presence of the lady with the black hair. They seemed to come hand-in-hand; it was on a day that I had to go into the village of Holywell and I had to go to the bank and pay some bills. The cashier started to chat to me and it was then she noticed my address. "How are you finding your new home?" she asked me.

"It's been hard," I told her. "Winter was not kind and we are all exhausted, to the point where I think we need a holiday!"

"I grew up in the red brick house at the top of your driveway," she told me. "It was the old vicarage then," she continued. "I didn't like it there growing up as the place was haunted by an old lady." Then she shocked me when she continued to describe what I had seen in the fireplace glass front.

I told her that I had seen this lady in our new home; she looked at me and told me that she was a depressing soul and no one could move her on, even though many had tried. "She brings misery and disaster to all whom she haunts."

"Dear God," I said to this woman, "thanks for that!"

She smiled and told me, "Good luck, as everyone only lasts 12 months in that house, then leaves with no money and broken marriages."

It was right about now I was wishing I banked with a different bank. I had left the house for a quiet shopping trip and left the shopping centre depressed. Things went from bad to worse over the next few months. Chris spent a lot of time in his room, Ray and I would be permanently grumpy with each other and Ray's back took a turn for the worse and he was rushed into hospital for emergency spinal surgery. What a nightmare this place was turning out to be; it was one disaster after another.

Then it happened; what had been a very lucrative job took a dive! Literally, as I worked in property when the property crash of 2007 hit, so did my income. Everything went from bad to worse and we were forced to make the decision to leave our home and come back to the Wirral. My mum also made a decision to go into sheltered accommodation as she was feeling on good form now after spending nearly seven years living with us. Her health had improved and she felt this would be the right move for her, under the circumstances.

Everything seemed to move pretty fast; I still owned two properties on the Wirral: my beautiful house in Moreton, which I loved so much and a little rental bungalow that I bought as an investment. I gave my tenant her notice and we moved back to Wirral would you believe exactly 12 months to the week in November 2007. I couldn't believe it – everything that woman in the bank had told me was happening. The property crash had meant that most of my properties were now not worth anything near what I had paid for them, so the saddest thing happened, after 20 years of hard work I lost everything, and I was declared bankrupt.

I was devastated. Everything was gone and now I also had to move out of the house in Moreton into my small bungalow, as the bankruptcy court took everything from us. I was so very unhappy and wondered so many times what I was meant to learn from all of this devastation.

Our life became simple in our little bungalow. I was so very unhappy at first, but then realised that things had become peaceful and quiet with space to contemplate what on earth had just happened to us.

It is only now as I write this book that my angels and guides are telling me the whole story, as for years I have been left in the dark.

You see I was never meant to move out of my lovely family home that my husband Ken and I had bought together. I was supposed to stay there, that place felt more like home than anywhere I have ever been in my life; we loved it and I still miss that house today.

The turmoil that happened in Halkyn with the ghost and the misery was their way to move us out and bring us back to the right road, as we had clearly steered from our pathway in a big way. My angels now talk to me every day and have enlightened me on the haunting at the farm in Wales. It was the ghost of a lady who had haunted that house and the house at the top of the hill; she had done so for many years, she had been desperately unhappy when she was alive, her husband was a mean man and her life was full of tears and despair.

When she passed, she didn't go to heaven as most do, she stayed where she knew best and grew heavier and heavier. Bringing misery and darkness to everyone who lived in that house, I have been told by Angel Michael that the blue orbs which were seen on a regular basis within our property were the angels and they and only they could help us with the doom and gloom that was surrounding us. They tried very hard to make me see what was happening but in those days, I wasn't listening. They kept her at bay, he told me, until I realised we must leave.

To this day I know that she is still there, reaping havoc on anyone who lives in that property. That space is hers and I believe that only a very strong person will convince her otherwise and manage to move her on into the light. That is where she needs to be, to rest in peace and I truly hope this person comes along one day and sets that lady free.

This move had now put me on the right track; I was back in Wirral and ready for my next part of my very important journey with the angels and my spirit guides.

You see, nothing is a coincidence; everything, even bad things, sometimes happen so you are brought back onto the right pathway, to continue your life's journey. Our move here to this little farm on the lanes was our destiny. I always knew I was destined to move to a farm but I had read the signs wrongly and had thought it was the Welsh farmhouse that was calling me.

Spirits talk to us every day but we don't always listen; the lesson here in this chapter is that if something is going so wrong, then don't try in desperation to fix it, perhaps it just isn't part of your life's plan, just take a deep breath and let it go.

NINE

Our New Home

It was October 2011. My friends who had lived in the farm on the lanes, not far from the lighthouse where my sister used to walk me as a child, had split up. Their marriage had broken down and they had gone their separate ways. Anthony had contacted me to see if there was anyone I knew that would want to move into the bungalow. He was tied into a long lease and would have to buy himself out if he didn't find someone to take on the lease. I nearly fell over myself getting to the farm. "I want it," I told Anthony. "I am destined to live here."

"It is falling to pieces," he told me. In fact, he called it a cash guzzler. It needed all sorts doing to it and he told me that the landlord did nothing to help them all the years they were there. I didn't care; the voices in my head made it a priority to get me into that house. I contacted the landlord and told him I would take on the lease. There was one small problem…I hadn't yet told Ray.

I am a very impulsive person and when I know I need to hurry believe me I run like the wind. Before we knew it, I had signed the papers and the new 3 year lease belonged to me. Ray was not a happy bunny; he couldn't believe I had done this without talking to him first but he soon got over it. The landlord was fabulous. He gave us three months' rent free for us to do up the bungalow and bring it back to life.

It was like a scene from that TV program Ground Force! All my friends came around in their work clothes and got stuck in – taking one room each we went through the bungalow and decorated, re-carpeted and fixed what was broken. Before we knew it, the place looked like brand new. I was so very excited to be bringing my horse Serene home at last to where I vowed she would see out her last days.

I would never have to bow to a landowner again. Serene was safe and no one could make her ill again.

We moved into the bungalow in November 2011. It was freezing cold, as the boiler had been broken for over 10 years. We managed to get most of the work done, but the money allocated to us was just not enough for a new boiler. It was so painfully cold that first winter. We managed somehow to get ourselves to spring without freezing to death but it had been a long hard slog. I contacted the owner and asked him to put a new boiler in, which he graciously did, so we have been warm ever since.

Although the house was now fully installed with new radiators and a brand new boiler, there were parts of the house that still remained cold. There had been no heating on in here for over 10 years so I just thought the walls had held onto the cold and were going to take some time to warm up. But this was not the case; in a previous chapter and when my friends lived in this bungalow, I mentioned that my mum had seen the spirit of a lady at the bottom of the hallway. I felt her in the house on numerous occasions; she felt lovely, calm and kind. I wasn't sure how to deal with her, as I had never helped anyone to enter the light before, so we just lived together in the same house. Although this lady was a kind spirit, sometimes I could feel a heavy darkness in the home.

If you saw where our bungalow was situated you would understand why it was a little spooky at times. It is pitch black, there are no streetlights as we live out of the way and off the main road down a country lane. However, spooky it certainly was. Once I had started my spiritual development class, I was able to connect with this spirit lady and find out some more about her. She was a lady who had lived on these lanes many years ago; she loved children but could never have her own, so when the children were about, so was she.

I have suffered with osteoarthritis since I was in my thirties and sometimes the pain in my hands is terrible. I would put them under my pillow to keep them warm. Some nights, I would awake at the gentle touch of someone tucking my hands into the bed covers, I would feel her hands on mine as she pulled over the duvet so my hands didn't get cold. At first this was a little eerie, but somehow comforting; she would move through our home as quiet as a mouse.

There were a few times on walking down the long corridor towards my bedroom that I would feel a not very pleasant sensation behind me. It was as if someone had run up behind me, then stopped dead.

This would frighten me, but I didn't know who it was. I knew this wasn't the little old lady, as she was beautiful and kind and this felt like a dark figure whose features I couldn't make out. This was a male and he knew I was frightened!

Ray had gone away for a few days with his father. I had run myself a lovely hot bath and as I stepped into the bathroom I felt something push past me. It took my breath away. "Who's there?" I asked. I felt nothing. 'Oh, it's my imagination', I thought and I continued to get undressed to climb into my lovely hot bath. The lights in the bathroom flickered off, which was scary as there are no windows in this bathroom so when the lights went off, it was pitch dark. I have learnt to light a candle now as we do have power cuts here regularly.

I climbed into the bath and lay back to have a nice soak and then all of a sudden the dark figure appeared. I nearly died! "Get out!" I shouted. "Get out of here! You are not welcome. Leave my house and don't come back!"

I felt the shift and he had gone, but had he? I spoke to Ray on the mobile that evening and told him about my ordeal. I am sure he thought I had completely lost it. "Are you ok now?" Ray asked.

"Yes I am fine, he has gone," I replied, then Ray hung up and I went to bed. I am sure you have guessed it by now but this dark figure had not gone. As soon as I hung up from Ray there he was and there he stayed, all night, in and out of my bedroom terrifying me.

It was on the third night when I just couldn't take anymore. I begged the angels to come and help me. They told me what to do as they said I must deal with this myself. "We will be at your side Lynn," they said.

"You must close your eyes and imagine you can see a roadway leading up to the heavens; at the end of the road is a large doorway, the light is shining brightly through the door. You must tell the earthbound spirit to step onto the road and head towards the light."

"And what if he won't go?" I asked.

"He will, but you must be strong with him and don't take no for an answer."

I closed my eyes and did all that I was instructed to do. To my amazement, I saw two figures step onto the pathway, one was the little old lady and the other was a tall man who was dressed from head to toe in black. He had a long black coat on and black boots. He looked like one of the three musketeers. They both headed to the doorway hand in hand. On reaching the door, they both turned to me and thanked me for showing them the way home. It was very emotional and within an instant, they had gone.

The house felt immediately different, very calm and warm. This beautiful bungalow now felt like home to me as it had felt so dark for the whole year before.

It was around 12 months later, the man dressed in black came back to me one day. He felt so very different; I could see his face and he no longer frightened me.

"I would like to thank you, Lynn," he said. "I would like to thank you for setting me free; I was able to see my family again whom I have been separated from for hundreds of years. You see Lynn, I was a smuggler, I worked with many off the shores of Wirral. We would wait for nightfall and with the shallow waters around here the small boats could come in easily without running aground," he said. I listened in amazement. "The aristocracy around the area used to head up the smuggling ring; they would gain much by this, however a lot of men lost their lives in treacherous seas and a lot of our souls stayed and wandered the shoreline for many years. The trouble was, the longer we stayed here, the harder it became. Being earth-bound was no joke; we felt heavy and grumpy, everything was very difficult but we didn't know what else to do."

What a story, I thought, and he continued.

"I am truly sorry for frightening you and your family and many families before, being a lost soul here made us dark and frightening and for this I am sorry. I hope you can forgive me." I smiled and told him it was ok. I had learnt a lot from him being here in my home. Some teachings I would never forget and I am sure I will come across more earth-bound spirits that need some guidance to find their way home, back to God and their loved ones.

It was nice for him to return and tell me his story and I know now that he is safe with all his descendants where he will continue his journey.

TEN

A New Beginning

My daughter Nicky, who is my eldest child, was a very troubled soul from the age of around seven. Two things happened around this time in her life, both as devastating as the next. It was just before Nicky's seventh birthday we lost our lovely dad and this knocked Nicky's world immensely as she adored her grandfather. The second thing was her father had left us. Nicky being only 7 years old and David was 3 years old. All this happened in the same week; what a blow to all of us that month of April had been. After she lost her granddad and as soon as she was old enough, Nicky at every opportunity has found mediums to visit looking for just a glimpse of her granddad.

I think Nicky's attraction to mediums was God's way of communicating with her young mind. As I had stopped listening to my voices, I'd switched off such a long time ago. This was to change about a year after my father's passing, this too was God's way of drawing me back in from the dark place in which my heart and my head were choosing to be. I know that God and the angels were trying to communicate with Nicky and sometimes I feel if only to get through to me via her. She would also hear her calling but didn't know quite what to do about it all.

Many years had passed and Nicky had children of her own, two in fact, my grandson Joe was around twelve years old, and my granddaughter Brogan was around two. There was a hairdresser that Nicky liked to go to not far from home. The girls there had seen a medium and they said she was amazing. Nicky phoned me asking if I would go with her to see her; I wasn't very keen on the idea. In fact, I did say no a few times before I gave in and agreed.

She asked me if she could have the readings here at my house. "Not a chance," I told her. I don't want anyone here.

"Please Mum," Nicky said. "She only comes to people's houses." Anyway, as you might expect, she ended up talking me into it. In the days leading up to the reading I was quite excited and I thought that perhaps now is the right time to do this again, as it had been many years since I had been to anyone. Nicky also informed me that I had to phone this lady and book a date with her to come.

The phone call was quite a strange one to be honest; I felt as if I was talking with someone that I had known for a while. "I am glad you phoned," she said. "I have been thinking of you, I have been told you are just like me but you need to be convinced of it before you will realise it is true and spirit can work with you."

Barbara had said much the same to me some years

before. "You are a healer, Lynn," she would say, "and you will help many people in years to come." Then, life took over. I had another child and I didn't pursue anything spiritual at all.

I told Ray that we had invited this lady to come. "I don't want to be here," he said.

"Oh well, that's good," I said. "We need someone to look after Brogan and who better than Granddad?" I smiled. Ray agreed after throwing me a look and off he went with our two-year-old granddaughter in tow. We lived by the sea, which on a nice day made for a lovely walk. Brogan was thrilled as granddad was definitely her favourite person in the whole universe.

Nicky and I were both excited but I didn't know where she would want to do our readings, where it would be quiet. Then I thought, why not sit on the couch in my bedroom as it is a huge room. Nicky and I decided that I would go first because my reading wouldn't be that long.

The doorbell rang and I answered the door. I don't know what I expected, to be honest. As I said earlier, I used to go to Barbara in Moreton about 2 miles away and she actually looked like a little gypsy lady and she was quite spooky. So, when I answered the door there was this very slim lady stood there; she was dressed a bit like me in a pair of jeans, nice blouse and jacket, a handbag over her arm. She had blonde bobbed hair, quite an attractive lady in her mid-fifties. She stepped in and gave me a hug. "Hi," she said, "my name is Liz. I heard your voice on the phone and I've been very excited about coming here today."

I smiled at her and thought I bet she says that to everyone! Why was I being such a sceptic? Had I grown into a non-believer? What on earth is wrong with me! I looked at her and thought to myself, 'She is a nice lady and has greeted you with a compliment, now behave', I told myself!

I asked her would she like a drink. She politely replied, "Yes please, I would love a glass of water." I introduced her to my daughter then the two of us left Nicky in my living room and we went and sat down on the couch in my bedroom.

She looked at me and told me that she didn't know why but she had been somewhat, well, sort of anxious about coming here today. I told her I felt the same to be honest. "Why do you think you were anxious?" I asked her. She said that she had got a feeling from me when I called her on the phone. "What kind of feeling?" I asked.

"A feeling that something special was about to happen," she said.

She asked the usual questions…had I had a reading before etc, and how long ago and then I told her what had happened. I told her about a reading I had 13 years ago. I'd been to a charity night to raise money for this poor little boy who was very ill. He needed to go abroad to have life-saving surgery. There were many mediums at this charity night and they all worked the floor individually picking out people to read. This woman with long scraggly hair picked me out of the crowd. The evening was held in Camel Lairds social club in Birkenhead, on the docks looking out over to the impressive Liverpool skyline on the opposite side of the famous River Mersey.

She just kept staring at me and I was thinking, 'Oh God'! as she came over. 'Please God, don't let her come to me'! She was singing this song that linked me to someone who had passed and who I'd rather not talk about in this book.

I knew she was the real thing because she couldn't possibly have had this person with her otherwise and then she mentioned my dad. "Dad watches over you Lynn," she said. "He is with you all of the time." Then all of a sudden she said, "I've got something to tell you that's not very nice."

"I don't want to know then!"

She said, "I have to tell you, it's important that you know this and it will become apparent why it is important." She told me that a friend would become pregnant and this friend would lose the baby; there was no way this baby would live no matter who intervened. This baby was never meant for the earth, this child would die before being born into our world. "Your job is to give a message to the parents of this child; this child has been received by God and is in God's kingdom."

I just gazed at her and asked, "What I am supposed to do with that information?"

She said, "It will become apparent." I was very upset as I didn't know who this would be or when. I hated the fact she said it and I was so upset because, about three months later two friends got pregnant at the same time. One was my business partner's wife and one was my best friend. For nine months I carried this knowledge thinking one of them is going to lose their baby, what was I to do? Should I say something? I was in such a dilemma – I became very stressed, so much so that I'm sure that's where my high blood pressure began.

My best friend's husband was in the navy fighting in Iraq. It wasn't an easy time all around. I was going backwards and forwards sitting with her thinking, is she going to be all right. She must have been five and a half or six months pregnant when I got a phone call to say Helen's been rushed into hospital, she's miscarrying the baby. She'd been taken to Liverpool Women's Maternity Hospital. I rushed over there; It was all a blur - I don't even remember how I got there.

It was a bank holiday so they had only a skeleton staff on duty in the hospital. I spoke to the doctor on my way into the ward. She is going through the process of miscarriage and there was nothing more they could do. I could hear my voices in my head; I just knew that this baby was not dead. "Has she been scanned?" I asked.

"No," they replied, "there is no technician on until tomorrow."

"WHAT?" I said angrily, "you haven't scanned her?"

"We have no one to do it," they said.

"Are you telling me that no one in the whole of this hospital knows how to use a scanner? How do you know she has miscarried? It could be something else."

I felt my blood pressure rising. "Do you know where her husband is?" I asked. "Well, he's fighting for this country, for your freedom, so I suggest you find someone who can scan her now." I was furious; how dare they just fob her off this way. Within 20 minutes, a doctor came from A&E and he said, "I do know how to use the scanner, but I'm not maternity."

I said, "It doesn't matter, just scan her." So they took her in to this room. "Come in with me Lynn," Helen said and as they scanned her, I stared at the monitor looking for signs of life. Then all of a sudden there it was; I burst into tears because there before my eyes was a strong heartbeat. Then this nurse said, "Oh, my God! This woman's not miscarrying – get her on to maternity…she is having a bleed!"

All was well. Had this been what that medium had seen? Helen and baby were fine, and she just needed to be watched over closely for the rest of her pregnancy. I left the hospital and headed home thinking, "Oh my good God, has what they told me just changed? Will this baby now be ok?" A million questions were racing around my head. But I had this overwhelming feeling that all would be fine.

Both couples were due to deliver their babies but I had no worries because I thought things had changed with the palaver with Helen and her baby. I was with my business partner when he got a phone call; I've got to go – my wife's has gone into labour. Little did I know but Helen by some weird coincidence had also gone into labour with her baby. Both went in at night and they both had their children on 18th October. Helen gave birth to a beautiful daughter and called her Rebecca whom I adore and am proud to say is my goddaughter, she's now 17.

My business partner's wife was carrying twins. The sequence of events from this night was so very devastating for the couple, the first one was born dead and had been dead for a good while, but the doctors had failed to notice. The second one only lived three days and then he also died. This absolutely knocked me for six – I couldn't believe how accurate this woman was apart from the fact it was two babies not one. I swore then 16 years ago I would never go to another clairvoyant again.

My business partner was heartbroken that their two boys had died.

So, I started shutting myself down from spirits completely. I didn't want to hear these things being told to me ever again. I didn't want them to speak to me, I was angry and upset, I shut my guides out and I shut God out.

I didn't listen; I started to ignore everything, it's as if I went on radio silence again for years. So now you understand why this woman coming to give Nicky and me a reading was such a big deal for me.

After telling this lovely lady my story, she sat and stared at me. "How very sad," she said. "I promise you, Lynn, I will not give you bad news; are you happy with that?" she asked me. I agreed and she continued.

She started off her reading by telling me about the phone call she'd had with me to make the booking. Her guides had told her, "You must go to this woman. There is something she needs to be told and you are the only link to her."

She pulled out this piece of paper with a half-moon of letters upon it, and then she brought out a dowsing crystal on the end of a silver chain.

"Oh my Lord," I thought, "she is going to do the Ouija board and in my bedroom!"

'It's ok', I heard in my head. Then I thought, 'Oh, it's just you being dramatic'. It was if I was looking for faults with her reading, to be honest, and then it happened. I saw her crystal spelling out 'Dad'.

"Have you got a dad in spirit?" she asked me in a quiet voice.

In my head, I was saying 'I am not going to tell you anything'. I was probably my own worst nightmare now I do my own readings. Then she said, "He's making a joke saying, 'Oh thank God, at last! I've been trying to make contact with you for years and you are just not listening to me'."

My eyes filled with tears, as I just knew that this lady had brought my lovely dad through and he was here on my couch in my dream home, talking to me.

He talked a little bit about me to her; he told her I was meant to heal, to bring closure to people like myself who had lost loved ones. Then he said Lynn would have been burnt at the stake for what she is capable of today, as healers where frowned upon by the church and were labelled witches! Dad then went on to say I was capable of more than I'd ever imagine. Liz laughed - then he said to her, "Liz, I don't know what you're laughing at, you'd have been right next to her."

I can't remember much of the reading to be honest; it was all about my spiritual journey and how it was about to be taken up a notch. He was saying how much he missed me because I'd shut him out for 13 years. He said, "I kept sending you signs."

I kind of knew the signs were coming from my dad but by shutting everybody else out and locking myself down, I'd shut my dad out too. I ended up in tears because I'd missed him so much.

"Please don't shut us out any more, you've got to listen – this is an important part of your life." To Liz, I will be eternally grateful, as she was brave enough to come to my home and awaken what was to be my true destiny.

Nicky had her reading and I don't know what went on with her as I was taking in what had just happened with me. Nicky enjoyed it and told me that she got a lot from her reading and thanked me for letting the lady come and see us at my home.

Before Liz left, she asked if she could come back and I agreed, before she left she said to me, "You should pursue this Lynn, don't let it go to sleep again because your dad is telling me that you are a very strong medium."

'Oh, really', I thought. "I've always been able to hear things, but I don't think I'm a medium."

She said, "My guides are telling me you must go to this woman."

So I asked, "How do you pursue it, how do you learn?"

She told me about a woman who lived locally to me, who runs a class. "She'll help you to develop your skills," she said. "I don't know if I still have her number, but I'll look for it when I get home; if not I know somebody who'll have it." I agreed I would follow my dad's wishes; Phyllis hugged me and left, leaving me a very happy lady.

As promised, Liz texted with a number to try. I felt very anxious. 'Am I really going to do this'? I thought, 'after all these years'. I heard a voice say, "Indeed you are, Lynn." Within those few hours, the floodgates had been opened and spirits were celebrating inside my head! There was not much sleep for a while after that afternoon.

I contacted the lady who was taking the development classes; she agreed to meet me and little did I know how quickly my life would move on from this meeting.

ELEVEN

My Spiritual Development

I remember driving up and down Leasowe Road many times over the past years and there was this bungalow on the left-hand side, just after the Leasowe Castle Hotel. I used to see this house and think how quaint it was and how it was like Hansel and Gretel's house from the fairy tale. It was very pretty and very welcoming but you must please remember the fairy tale, so did the house attract them and then it turned out to be something it wasn't!

It was a lovely house and set right back from the main road; it had a big veranda on the front and big carved wooden windows, with a little round window in the roof which looked like a porthole on a ship. I always wondered who lived there and how lucky they were.

On calling the lady who was hosting the development class, whose name was Pat, I realised when she gave me the address that this was actually where she lived. Was this a coincidence? Maybe, maybe not. I was very excited to meet this lady as I felt I could learn a great deal from her and her development group.

We made arrangements for me to visit and just before I left home, she sent me this message saying, "Just tap on the door then open the door and shout up; I will be upstairs." I found out when I arrived that she didn't own this house – she rented a flat in the roof. She had her kitchen downstairs and up a flight of stairs there was her living room and two bedrooms.

When I met her, I took an instant like to her; she was very gushing but seemed very nice. I'd have said she was about 65. She had this blonde wavy hair, a local accent, so was definitely born and bred around Merseyside. She made me feel very welcome and comfortable in her company. The set-up of her flat was quite strange as she had no windows which you could actually see out of. In her living room, there were two windows: one a velux roof window and one was a round window which was set into the side wall. There was stained glass in one of the windows which was of the lighthouse next to my house and if you looked through it you could see the lighthouse's outline and it was complete replica of it.

This window was beautiful and I knew when I saw this it was where I was meant to be, at least for now. The lighthouse has always been there since the start of this awakening and then of course I didn't know this at the time but spirits were to name my first book, 'A Light to Guide Us Home', with of course, the lighthouse in mind.

Pat told me that she did a group on a Monday night and would I like to start this coming week. I was so excited and my dad was pushing me. I was quite shut down when I first went there, as I didn't know what to expect and it wasn't until I started going there regularly, that I opened up to my gifts.

There were three ladies there plus the lady hosting the group, one lady was a friend of hers and had been going to her groups for over 8 years for development classes and I have to say I was thinking, 'What? 8 years! Gosh', I thought. 'I am going to take a lot of developing, aren't I'!

There was another lady called Jean who was gorgeous; she was retired. Everyone there seemed to be retired apart from the girl in the corner. She's was about 38 and from the other side of Liverpool. She had a long way to come, but she didn't seem to mind.

It was a new group starting, even though some had been to her groups before. Jean had been going for 6 years on and off and one lady for 8 years on and off. This girl and I were new. The evening started with a brief chat about our week and then we were asked to bow our heads and go within. I didn't know what 'go within' meant! I felt a bit of a numpty! She explained to me how to go within. "Close your eyes and take deep meaningful breaths, sit quietly in your own space and just be." she told me.

"We are going to do a meditation, you will hear my voice and I will take you on a journey but before we can do that we must open up, this means open all our chakras and let in the light of spirit." I could feel myself panicking. 'Oh Lord', I thought, but she talked us through it and it was actually quite easy.

Opening up is something I had never done before, probably because I didn't know what it was or what the benefits were. I have to say the first time I did this opening up I felt fine, the only thing was you were on another blinking planet - you did feel lighter and more observant, but if you left and you hadn't shut down you'd end up with a banging headache or just felt generally unwell because you were wide open to everything, every ghost walking past your house everything could get in. It was a bit of hit or miss at first. I used to think, 'Oh my God, I'm knackered all the time', because I hadn't shut down properly.

This shutting down I came to realise some years later was only something us newbies had to do and only because we would be bombarded by spirit, both earthbound and in heaven.

How I loved going to this group. I never missed a Monday night ever. It always made me feel so close to spirit when I attended this group. She used to charge £5 a head for the Monday night group, which I thought was really good. We would go over a lot of different things; she would show us how to be aware of different feelings, when spirits come close and how you felt when you opened yourself up and how you'd feel when you shut yourself down. She'd take us on these journeys and she'd tell us we can choose to meet with someone on the journey, so I'd call in my dad or other loved ones who had passed over, it was nice because they used to meet me there once I started going regularly. My loved ones knew that this was a place where they could contact me without a doubt, as someone in the group would pick up messages from them, even if I didn't.

My dad would stay with me every Monday and I would know he was there; it was amazing. Everyone should go and learn how to connect – it's something we all should be able to do. It's a natural thing to do;

society has made us frightened of what we don't know.

She would give us a pack of angel cards and show us how to read them. We would have to do readings for all the individuals in the room; doing this would be a good way to learn. We were never allowed to tell anyone about ourselves or it would hinder any readings they gave to us. Anyone who was given me to read would always get my dad, because he would always be really prominent in the room.

My gifts came on in leaps and bounds; the others in the room would compliment me and tell me I was a natural. I used to think they were nuts. I had been going now for over 12 months and I did feel as if this lady had become a good friend; we would go out to lunch or share an afternoon cuppa and a natter. I felt really happy.

It was here I heard again about the hands-on healing technique called Reiki Healing, which had helped my mother so many years before. It was no sooner those words came out of her mouth that my body buzzed with excitement, "I have to do it," I told her. 'This is for me', I thought. My every fibre was jumping for joy, spirits were elated. This was to be a part of my journey. Pat was a Reiki Master teacher, so this meant she could attune me,

I asked her, "How much is an attunement?"

"Around £85 for the first and £85 for the second."

'Gosh', I thought, 'I can't afford that'.

"I will help you," Pat told me, "and one day when you are in a better situation if you really wish to, you can pay me back."

"Really?" I asked.

"Yes," she said. Well, I couldn't believe my ears, I know now that Pat's guardian angel had something to do with that. She had whispered in her ear and asked her to help me. It was July 2014 when I had my Reiki Level 1; it was an amazing experience and I felt I had a lot of work ahead of me.

There were rumblings amongst the group, strange things had started happening during the evenings when we were there; we could all feel bad energies and I was getting nothing at all from the evenings. It was as if I had been switched off.

Then all of a sudden, my dad stopped coming, or so I thought. I now know that Dad was there but when Pat was opening me up, he was shutting me down and I stopped getting things. I stopped being able to read people or bring spirits through to give messages. Things started getting a bit strange. The explanation from Pat for this happening was that they give it to you really easily to start with, so that it gives you confidence, then they take it back slowly and you've got to work for it harder. Well, I felt this didn't make much sense, but I was new to all this so who was I to argue?

I did wonder why my dad had gone quiet, as he was my encouragement. I never thought about it at the time but it was only twelve months down the line. I realised what was going on and I did struggle with it. But every now and then I'd switch on and I'd give a really good reading to someone in the room. Everyone was mesmerised and they always wanted me to do their readings but the more they wanted me to do the readings, the more Pat got cross in the corner. She'd give encouragement then shoot you down in flames. I wondered what on earth was going on; this lovely lady's personality had changed dramatically.

She used to be horrible to the girls, she'd snap at them and it was as if she had a split personality. She'd teach you how to do a reading then you'd produce it then she'd contradict what she'd told you to do. She'd make you work hard for what you had, but she was nasty about it, she was never satisfied about what you were doing. This wasn't the person I had met over 18 months ago, what on earth was going on!

I have to say I learnt the hard way and was taught to go the extra mile for my clients and all this came from Pat. She would push me for more details. "It's not good enough Lynn," she would say. "just to say I have a woman in the room, anyone can do that! Describe them!"

Before I knew it I could tell you what colour eyes they had or how tall they were, which I have got Pat to be thankful for because of her I did push myself and always expected more than from my readings than most mediums would give. Sometimes you'd give all that information to her and then spirit would start showing you objects. 'Oh God, they're giving me a red car or a red flower', and I would know which flower it was or they'd show big hands or show me a boat and always something that connected the diseased person to the person sat with me. It was amazing and I was so excited at what I had learned.

When you contact spirits, it's all suggestion and pictures and you have to string it all together, that's why it's exhausting. You have to work hard just to string one sentence together. Pat was a good teacher, until I got too good, then she started getting cross with me. I do know now why this was happening, there had been a new girl start in the group and every time she opened up, it was like she was possessed. She would be channelling earth-bound spirits that were in Pat's house. But she didn't know she was doing it and Pat, who should have been helping her to shut down or move them on, seemed to enjoy watching this girl. Her tone would change, her mannerisms would change, she was frightening to look at, it was like the lights were on, but there was nobody there. Pat used to encourage her and of course the spirits that were coming through her loved every minute of it because they were gathering energy from her and getting stronger and stronger each week. If you ever went out with Pat for lunch or met at somebody else's house she was a different person. It was strange because she would change right back to this aggravated woman when she was back in that flat. Something wasn't right, something was getting to Pat and we were not experienced enough to deal with it.

Monday night group had been cancelled just for one week, as Pat had gone to her sister's in Sheffield, so after chatting amongst the group, I invited them around to my house for a girly night so that we could fill our empty Monday evening.

It was a lovely summer evening and we had a couple of glasses of wine and some food for supper. They all agreed and arrived about 7 pm. We had such a lovely time. I got actual footage of the orbs and the angels in the room.

My black cat had come in to let us all know that spirits were about. There were loads of orbs everywhere and the air seemed to be filled with electricity. We were all asking questions of the orbs and they were answering. In my experience, it's always been my dad, Christopher's dad or the angels. They're balls of energy; the girls were all shrieking, they couldn't believe it! They had never seen anything like it and in all the years they had been working with spirits.

I had been turning one of my bedrooms into a workroom for me to do my readings and my Reiki healings. I was nearly finished and before I knew it, my next step on my spiritual journey was to begin. I brought them in to look at the room and they all thought that the energy in this room was gorgeous; it was just right for what I had in mind.

Then we got on the conversation of what was going on in Pat's house. We were all in agreement that something untoward was going on and how she was different when she was in there, and she was getting down and tired and ill all the time. We decided we would talk to her to see if we could get somebody in to clear it. Two of the ladies had known Pat a long time and they told me they had never seen her so grumpy and fed up.

We all thought a lot of her and we thought we'd like to help find someone in to clear the space and then she would be ok. There was a lady that everyone seemed to know, this is what she was clearly put here for, to help with the clearing of negative energies out of houses, or helping earth-bound spirits to move on to where they should be. This all sounded fabulous to me; I had grown very fond of Pat and I would do anything to help her.

Well, clearly after the next turn of events we realised that there was a bit of a two-faced person in the camp and it was made to look as if we were scheming against her. What she didn't realise was that there was a lot of love in that room for her that night and it was all with good intention; we just wanted to help. We all thought the world of her, she clearly had a split personality when she was in that house and it got massively blown out of proportion. This other woman said, "Lynn's after taking your groups off you and having them in her house." Which was hilarious, as I just about knew what I was doing.

That had never been my intention, ever, although I am being asked now if I'll start groups. Spirits tell me 3 years on since that night that I have a lot to teach and the more light that is brought into this world the better, so it's funny how things actually turn out. People want to develop themselves, they realise that there is something more out there than what they are already capable of. The help we were intending to give to Pat, all five of us, not just me, definitely backfired on us, but did it? You see, it blew up massively – there was a big fallout. She blamed me for everything even though there were five of us there that evening. Pat fell out with me, but not the others. I found that very upsetting indeed. She still sees the others and they never really fell out and to this day, I'll never know why I got the blame.

It wasn't until my guides told me that she was being cleared out of my life and that I was not meant to be around her or her group and that she was the first of a massive clearing. The guides told me that these people also were not meant to be in my life; this incident started off a chain of events which you will find hard to believe. The funny thing is that Pat told me herself that when you choose the Reiki pathway, negative people will be cleared out immediately as

Reiki healing is pure and spirits will not allow your journey to be tainted by anyone.

Let me tell you, five people had been snatched away from me; each one of them was a big shock and all because I'd chosen my Reiki path. Some people I had called my friends were exposed to me as frauds and spirits moved people out of my way and they left my life, never to return.

This sounds rather drastic but let me tell you, life has become beautiful since all this happened. I am where I am meant to be and spirit work is at my side daily. I am happy and I am content and I wish everyone, even those I mysteriously fell out with, love, light and happiness in abundance.

Things began to change for me then and I would hear things much clearer. At night, I could hear the sound of the earth spinning on its axis; there were high vibrations in the room and this noise was on a different frequency all together. It's like changing your radio frequency and tuning into God.

It was never my intention to start my own group at this time as I realised I had much to learn, so I set out to find myself a new teacher. I found a lady in Moreton and she was well established. She had been a spiritual teacher for a long time. I had heard Pat talk of her but she always talked as if she didn't know her. So, I was surprised when I met this lady that she had actually taught Pat when Pat had started out. What a turn up for the books that was! I have learnt a lot from the groups, which I have attended over the years and one lesson I have learned the hard way; no matter what work you are doing, jealousy can always creep in. Little did I know that the new group would also bring me feelings of isolation and there were times I wondered why I bothered at all? 'Was this a lesson from spirits', I would think to myself; the answer always came back to me the same.

"Lynn, you need no one to teach you how to be yourself; those who make you feel sad are also on their own journey. They have many lessons to learn, as do you, but you know, don't you Lynn, that those who upset you and push you away, do so because they cannot cope with the brightness that you carry along in your soul. Do not feel that these things are injustices done to you; think of them as a message from us, telling you that you don't need to be there," said Raoul.

I always had my teachers on a pedestal when it is spirits I should have had up there, not the living. I feel that people are taken in by others and the people who this lady was dealing with where I was told working in the darkness also and practising things I did not want to be involved with.. This is not only a lesson for me but for the teacher as some of the people she deals with are not all they seem to be and one day this will become apparent to her, but yes you have guessed it this will be the hard way as lessons must be shown to us and people will always show their true colours in the end.

Part of my work with this lady was something called the Priestess course. She has a magical way of bringing spirit to us and some of the work we have done is with the spirit of Mary Magdalene. These stories, of which there are many, are part of my next book, which will be called 'Our Angels and Guides'. This book will show you everything I have learnt in detail.

TWELVE

When Spirit Takes Over

This has to be the hardest part of my book to write; my son had difficulties from the very first day he drew breath. You see, my youngest son had the most traumatic of births; he was born with the cord around his neck. This was terrifying as it was wrapped around many times; he was born after many hours of labour but he had been almost strangled by his cord.

The birth was horrific and I think that they realised he should have been born by a caesarean. But it was all too late as by the time the hospital realised what had happened he was already in the birth canal and was suffocating. He was literally dragged from my body and the resuscitation team were on standby.

They managed to bring him around and told me all was ok. He had a few bruises on his body due to the trauma and what looked like rope marks around his neck, but it would all clear and he was a strong healthy boy. You may be wondering why I am telling you this story; it will all become clear and how a miracle was given to a desperate mother and how it had an impact on 20 years of a young person's life.

The truth is, he was far from ok. My poor boy always looked so sad, from a very young age he wouldn't speak to anyone and struggled with socialising. Even as a 1-year-old he would panic at the thought of going anywhere he didn't know, even a trip to the shops or sometimes family get together proved terrifying for him. He didn't sleep for longer than a couple of hours at a time; this was exhausting for everyone in the household, as he would scream as if he was terrified.

I had taken him to the doctors more times than I care to mention; when I look back it was all so very frightening. The doctors came to the conclusion for the next 4 years of his young life, that he was just a naughty child! I think that was their answer for 'we don't know what's wrong with him'!

Both his father and I were at our wit's end; we just didn't know what to do. You should have seen my son – he was so beautiful, with the face of an angel, he had white blond hair and the darkest brown eyes. He was such handsome little boy but his soul was so troubled. I would hold him tight and tell him 'it will be ok, Chris I promise, if I could take this away from you I would but I don't know how'.

He didn't have many friends growing up but there was one specific family who lived in the road opposite ours where he would make a special bond. Their young boy was exactly the same age as Chris and they got on very well. Chris didn't seem to mind going to their house and playing when he was young; they grew up together and both started school at the same time. Tracy, Michael's mum was on his list of trusted adults.

My best friend Helen also had a son who was two years younger than Chris and because I saw so much of Helen, Chris and Mike became lifelong friends. Helen was very intuitive. She was such a good person to have around you, and we complimented each other perfectly. We have been the best of friends for over 40 years now and we will continue beyond into the next chapter of our lives and once our life here has finished.

Christopher's school years were a disaster, he couldn't endure school; the anxiety was building and building inside my little boy. Somehow, he managed his way through his first school, but towards his 8th birthday things seemed to be getting worse. The classes were too big and it was all just too much for him. Without a doubt, his education was suffering.

It was at this time that we decided that it would be a good idea to look for a smaller school, or private education. We found a school in Hoylake on the Wirral and Chris began the happiest of his school years there. He made friends with a boy called Jim, who came from a lovely family who lived close by. Jim became another of Christopher's lifetime friends, his family have always treated Chris as if he were one of their own. Nothing was ever too much trouble and in my lovely friend Carol (Jim's mum), I have much to be grateful for.

I don't know how Chris managed to get through to his 16th year in school but finally that year came and with it the stress of his final exams. As you can imagine, he didn't do very well at all, but God love him he decided that he would continue his education and go to sixth form college. He seemed to be happy at the college and it was less formal than his school years. He started to flourish and enjoyed the college very much. He met a nice girl there who seemed to match Chris completely. She wasn't pushy and realised that Chris didn't want to do all the things the other lads were doing, partying till morning, drinking, smoking etc. He just wasn't interested.

Then tragedy struck, Christopher's dad and I had separated a couple of years before. I always loved Chris's dad from the bottom of my heart but he had his own issues; he had come from a very difficult childhood, his mum was abused by his dad, and his father was a heavy drinker.

He came from a big family: five boys and five girls. The boys seemed to inherit the father's drink problems, thankfully that was all that Chris's dad inherited. He was a kind and loving man and he loved me with every breath in his body, but the drink was a problem.

I always heard a voice saying he must stop, he must stop. His dad died at quite a young age with cancer of the stomach due to excess drinking through his life. I begged my husband to stop drinking but he couldn't and I know now that drink was his hiding place, as he too couldn't cope with people.

Christopher never lost touch with his dad, although the breakup was very painful for all involved. I thought that if I gave his dad the ultimatum to stop drinking or we wouldn't last, that he would stop. But that never happened. It was very sad as I loved him so much; hearts were broken when we split.

Things went from bad to worse and our breakup

had gone too far so we never got the chance to reconcile the marriage. I think we were both as stubborn as each other. I do know that neither of us wanted this, to split up a family is not an easy decision. But we eventually divorced and sadly all was lost.

I met my husband Ray about 3 years after Ken and I split. I know it's hard for a child as no man can replace their father but Ray is a kind man and has always treated me well and we have been married now for seven years.

It was one cold November morning and there was a knock at the door; Ray went to answer the door and I was sitting in the living room at the back of our little bungalow. As Ray walked up the hallway, that voice in my head told me to take a deep breath. I felt a panic come over me; I didn't even know who was at the door but I knew something was terribly wrong. I heard a familiar voice, it was a friend of mine and Ken's. As soon as I heard her voice, I jumped up. I ran into the hallway where she stood looking at me. "Lynn, something terrible has happened."

I burst into tears. "Where is he," I said, "what has happened to him?" Without her saying his name, I knew she had come to tell me something about Ken. What came out from her lips next will stick with me for eternity.

"I am so sorry Lynn, Kenny was found dead 3 days ago!" I just broke down. "No!" I cried. "My boy, what I will tell him?"

I lost control and was hysterical. "This will kill him – what happened?" I asked. She continued to tell me that he had been ill and told no one; he walked out from hospital, went home and died in his bed. He had been diagnosed with stomach cancer but it was all too late, it had taken over his body and there was nothing the hospital could do for him.

I was devastated and I just didn't know how I was going to break this news to Chris. The anxiety in him was already very prominent, this would just be so distressing to him.

Chris had already gone to college. I phoned college and told them what had happened and that I would be sending his stepfather to bring him home. How do you tell any child one of their parents has tragically died? My heart was racing as I heard the front door open. Chris and Ray walked in and I don't remember a worse moment ever, than when I had to tell my son that his father was gone. He took the news very quietly, stood up and went to his room.

The next days passed quickly, Chris, as one might predict, was growing increasingly quiet. We pushed through these weeks tenderly and with the funeral over, he went back to college. He was surprisingly calm, but my voices where telling me different, and to be aware there was something happening in the quiet of Christopher's mind. I kept a close eye on him, making sure not to smother him. Then the terrible day came I had a call from college to tell me no one could find Chris. He had signed into college in the morning but hadn't turned up to class.

The teachers were aware of what had happened and also that he suffered with severe anxiety, so alarm bells rang when he was missing from class. I called and called Christopher's mobile phone but he wasn't answering. I was worried sick...where could he be? I got in my car and went looking for him. Where would he go? My mind was chaos and I couldn't think straight; because of his anxiety, he couldn't use buses or most public transport, so I figured he would be heading home on foot.

I couldn't find him anywhere then he answered a text. 'Come and get me, Mum'. That's all it said. I found him on the main road heading home. He wouldn't speak when I picked him up he just said, 'Take me home please', and nothing more. I called the college and told them he had been found. This was just towards the end of the year. He had taken his exams for that year and had A+ with distinction. I was so very proud of all his hard work. But that day he walked out from college would be the last time he would ever return.

Christopher's anxiety had taken over his mind and body. His father's tragic death had pushed our son over the edge and the years that were to follow would forever stick in my mind.

On that day in 2010 my lovely son took to his room and didn't come out again for 3 years! His anxiety had consumed him completely. We tried everything to bring him back into the real world but nothing could convince him that there was anything out there that was worth his time. He didn't see friends or family; he had isolated himself from everyone except myself and my mum. His bond with Nan was unbreakable. She loved him so much, that every time she visited he would break the mould and come downstairs to see her. The doctors told me Chris was grieving and I was to let him do so in his own way but anxiety and grief was not a good combination. Chris lived in the dark, he had lost a lot of weight through his illness and things just escalated.

I had been through some terrible financial

problems, as during the property crash of 2007/8 I had lost a lifetime's work and all my savings and income from twenty years of hard work. This had left us in financial ruin, but my guides and angels where telling me to go get it, this house is for you and you must move quickly.

To say heaven and earth were moved in order for us to move here is definitely an understatement! I was told it was here that Chris would recover; 'Do everything in your power, Lynn, this house is meant for you'. I thought my voices were absolutely nuts! How could I afford this house? Where was the money coming from to pay a rent that was so far out of my reach?

So many questions – I felt as if my head would explode! Spirits guided me every step of the way, although at this time in my life I still wasn't aware of who I could hear in this head of mine. But nevertheless I went ahead and took a massive step and went after that bungalow with what felt like the force of the heavens behind me. 'You have work to do there', I heard a voice say, 'now move yourself you have no time to waste'.

I found a tenant for my little bungalow and we moved out of there into the little farm in November 2011.

The house was not the most inviting place to be it was always cold and dark. As I said in a previous chapter, I would feel a dark presence in there every time I entered the house. I could feel there were a few earth-bound spirits in this house and one or two of them were dark and depressing. At this time I didn't know how to clear them away. I recall one time when the other people lived here the lady was having some sort of get together. She invited me and Mum, my mum was in a wheelchair in those days as her hips were very bad.

My friend's husband had made a ramp for us to get Mum into the house in her chair. We pulled up at the house and he was waiting for us at the door. The two of us pushed Mum up the ramp into the vestibule. The hallway to farm was like a runway. It was very long with all the rooms running off either side. At the bottom of the hallway my friend had a computer desk. On entering the house, we could see their sons on the computer at the bottom of the hall. My mum smiled and said hello to them. The evening went well, and if I remember rightly it was some sort of Tupperware party.

My friend's husband helped Mum down the ramp again at the end of the evening and into my car. On the journey home Mum turned to me and said, "Well that was a little strange." I asked her what she meant. "Why didn't the lady who was with the children come into the party?"

"What lady?" I asked.

"The lady who was with the boys at the end of the corridor?" I turned to Mum, and with an astonished look on my face said, "There was no lady in the corridor," I told her.

"There was," she said crossly at me. "I smiled and said hello as we arrived there and she smiled back at me," Mum continued.

"I saw no one," I told Mum, "but I will phone my friend and see what she says." I did make that phone call to a very surprised friend. There was no one here but those in the room with us she told me. It was then we realised my mum had seen the spirit of a lady and on describing her to the neighbours and people who had lived in the lanes a long time, they told us that she lived in a little house here before she passed. We moved into the farm and Chris was excited as it was to give him so much freedom. The bungalow was set in five acres of land, right on the sea front. Chris would heal here, I was told by spirits, 'but it will take time, just trust in what we tell you'.

The first twelve months were difficult; there were a lot of repairs to do and also things were very difficult with money. However, we struggled through and made it work. I was very happy to have my beautiful horse outside my window again. This is the life I thought; things have got to get better here. We were sent here for a reason, now I had to find out what that reason is.

Things didn't quite go as I thought. Chris went from bad to worse and in our lovely new home his life became darker and his anxiety seemed to have consumed him. Over the next couple of years, Christopher's anxiety got so bad he stopped coming out of his room at all until we were in bed or out of the house.

I had spoken to doctors about him and they tried to get through to him but to no avail. I was worried for his life; he had lost about three stone in weight, his skin was pale and his body was weak. He had given up on life, at the age of 18 years he told me he was finished. "I am no good, Mum. Who would want me? I can't breathe when others are around." "What is the use?" he would ask me, "what is the use?"

To hear these words coming from the mouth of your child is the most painful experience ever. I would hold him tight and tell him it will be ok Chris I promise, if I could take this away from you I would but I don't know how. My own stress levels were through the roof; my blood pressure was terrible and nothing seemed to stabilise it. As Chris got worse, my heart was breaking in two.

I felt so alone. Although I had family around me, my sisters and my brother had their own lives to think about, so Christopher's troubles were not foremost in their minds. I know this wasn't intentional but I really don't think they ever understood the devastating torment that both Chris and I were going through and sometimes it felt as if we were going through it alone.

It was then I started to ask my father who had died many years ago for help and I begged Ken, Christopher's dad, to help our boy. 'I don't know what to do', I would cry. 'I am going to lose him. Please someone help us'! The desperation had taken over me now and I felt bad things happening.

The last straw was the day Chris locked himself in his bedroom and barricaded the door. His cousin, whom he loved like a sister, was here with the horses. I shouted to her to come and help me to speak to Chris. He told us both to go away. He never let me into his room, he kept it dark and I would leave his food at the door.

This was a desperate situation. I had tried to get in but he wouldn't open the door. "Please Mum just go away, leave me alone." I felt something really bad would happen this day if I just walked away. I threw myself at the door breaking the lock and Tania and I pushed the door open. He was very upset at what I had just done but I was so very glad we had done this as I think he had given up that day. I don't want to think what would have happened if I had just walked away.

I heard a voice telling me it would be ok – he has a friend around the corner. As you can imagine, I had no time for these voices; I thought I was going mad!

I made a phone call to the doctor; our usual doctor wasn't there, so I asked for any doctor to come visit him as I thought that he was now in a desperate state of mind.

It was around 3 hours later when I heard a knock at the door. A young Indian man stood on the doorstep; I opened the door and he stepped inside. I asked him into the living room and we spoke for a while about Chris. "I cannot believe what I am hearing!" he said. "Why has this become so bad?"

I explained that Chris took to his room after losing his father and hadn't been in public since. The doctor was shocked to say the least. "I cannot allow this," he said with a sharp tone to his voice. "Please fetch him to me."

I explained that he hadn't seen anyone but me for 3 years and that it might take me a while to coax him out. I went to Christopher's door, which was locked from the inside. "The doctor is here, please come out," I asked him.

"No, Mum, I can't," said Chris. "Please Mum, ask him to leave."

"No," I said, "come out, or I am coming in!" I heard a click and the door unlocked. Chris came out and very sheepishly entered the living room.

The doctor looked shocked. "I cannot believe my eyes," he said. "You look so weak and terrified at the very thought of speaking to me." Then he stuck out his hand. "My name is Dr J and I am here to help you

Chris. Your mum has told me everything and I cannot allow this to happen to such a young life."

Chris shook the hand of the doctor and a smile came over his face. After a good chat, the doctor decided that meds where the way forward just to stabilise him. Chris shook his head, "I don't want tablets."

"These will help," the doctor said, "just give them a try. I will come back and see you in five days." Chris agreed and the doctor left while Chris went back to his room.

I heard a familiar voice say, 'Don't worry Lynn, don't worry'. I still didn't know quite who these voices were, I just knew they would help me as they have always done in my life.

I thought we had made a breakthrough. I felt very confident that this was the way out of his terrible situation. The doctor came back after the five days and made a pact with Chris. "I will see you every week," he told Chris. "Is that ok?"

"Yes," Chris replied with a smile.

"However, this is the last time I will come and see you at home."

Christopher's face dropped. "What do you mean?" he asked the doctor.

"You will come to me at the doctor's surgery." I could see the terror in Chris's face. "You will come every Monday when surgery is over. I will see you and pick up on your progress every week." Chris reluctantly agreed, however the first time he was meant to go I just couldn't get him to walk out of the front door. You see, he hadn't been out of the house in years and the thought of it sent him into a panic. The doctor yet again came to us. "This is the last time

Chris, I am a very busy man, do you understand?" he asked. "Please, you must try and come to me."

The next Monday came and Chris managed to get into the car and go to the doctors. I felt as if heaven and earth had moved for him that day. He had made the first step outside of the house. I knew this was not going to be a quick fix but it was the first step of many.

During these times, I asked for help from God and the angels every night, 'please help my son', I would ask. I would feel comfort in knowing my dad and Christopher's dad would be listening but frustration in the fact that I couldn't speak with them.

During one of his many trips to the doctors, I was called in the room with Chris to discuss the next step. The doctor told me that Chris hadn't had closure on his father's sudden passing and he said it was time to spread his father's ashes and put him to rest.

I did not have Ken's ashes – his brother had them. I had asked him not to spread the ashes before contacting me first, as this was Christopher's dad and I felt he should be present when this was done. I called his uncle and asked if we could have the ashes, as Chris needed closure. To my surprise he told me, "I am sorry, but I have done it already." I was shocked and upset at this as he had promised that he wouldn't do it without us. On reflection, I realise it must have been hard for him too, this was his brother and they were very close and it was now over 3 years since his death.

I had the awful task of having to inform Chris what had happened. He quietly stared at me and said it's ok, but I could see on his face that it was far from ok. The only consolation was that Ken's brother had told me that the ashes had been spread where they had all spent many a holiday fishing from the rocks on Anglesey.

This made Chris smile when I told him, as this was his dad's favourite place in the world. I told him that we could go visit and say our goodbyes to his dad one day and Chris agreed but time went on and still the only time Chris left the house was to go to the doctors. He never ventured out anywhere else, even with me in the car. He was still in that bad place where desperation could take over him quickly. I continually tried to get him to come out with me, anywhere, it didn't matter, I just continued to ask him and the answer was always 'NO'!

THIRTEEN

Chris's Awakening

It was a July morning, midweek if I remember rightly. I was awoken by the feeling of desperation. I cannot explain how that felt, only to say that I jumped out of bed thinking something was wrong with Chris. I flew up the corridor and to Christopher's room. I tapped on the door but no answer, so I opened the door with the excuse I was letting the cat out. Our big tom cat Tiger always slept with Chris from the minute we got him but always knocked on the door in the morning for me to let him outside.

On opening the door, I realised both the cat and Chris were fast asleep so I went and made myself a cup of tea and pondered on what on earth had woke me up. A friend was staying with us at the time in our spare room as she had broken up with her husband and was in-between homes. As if I didn't have enough on my plate here, I had said she could come and stay a while until she sorted herself out. I told her of this awakening that I had experience that morning and that it felt so real. As I was telling her, I could hear something or someone talking to me as clear as day.

'Get him out'! this voice was saying. 'Get him out'! Then it all came to my mind, as if someone had opened the floodgates to heaven and they were shouting to me: 'GET HIM OUT'! I was shocked by this as although I have heard voices all my life this was different. This was clear and precise. I looked at my friend and knew straightaway what I must do. "We have to go to Anglesey," I told her. "We have to go today."

She looked at me astonished, "Oh my God," she said. "We can't, he will be ill – he will have a panic attack!"

It was early in the morning and early morning was never a good time for Chris. I decided I would wait until around eleven and wake him up then and tell him what we were going to do today. I could hear a voice saying, 'It will be ok, Chris will come, he will be fine'. I felt sick to the bottom of my stomach! I woke Chris and let him properly come round before I told him of my plans.

I felt confident that what I was hearing was all going to go very smoothly and to plan. What they didn't inform me of was the reaction I was about to receive from my son.

He completely went into meltdown; he had a panic attack at the thought of jumping in my car and driving all that way. I was upset and Chris was in a right state!

Well, that didn't go as I thought it would, but there were no voices; all were silent.

I felt very much deflated, all that upset and I still hadn't got him out of the house. I spoke to him later that day; I told him I was sorry about the upset but this was something we would need to do, to move on in life. Chris being Chris, he was so understanding. He knew exactly what I was trying to do and also knew how much he was loved and that I only wanted what was best for him.

I went to bed that night feeling very emotional. I had watched my son all his life go through turmoil after turmoil. I was worn out, both emotionally and physically. I have to tell you, my prayers were very strong that night! I wanted to know why this was happening to my beautiful son, why God had forsaken this boy who had such a big heart and a beautiful soul.

The rest of the week went by pretty quickly. I went to bed Friday night feeling quite calm really and Chris had been sitting outside that afternoon with me and my friend in the gorgeous summer sunshine. He looked happy and carefree sitting there laughing with us. But of course, he was within the boundaries he had set for himself; he was in the safe zone.

It was around 4 am on Saturday morning I awoke with the same feeling I had experienced on that Tuesday morning. I sat up in bed feeling quite emotional, but this time I felt strong as if someone had lifted me up and given me an injection of strength. I got up out of bed and went to the kitchen to make some tea. It was a lovely morning and I opened the patio doors and watched the sun coming up over our beautiful home. It was surprisingly warm for that time of the day.

The birds were singing and for a moment I felt I didn't have a care in the world. A complete feeling of peace surrounded me and then it happened, the voice came back. 'It is today', they said. 'Prepare yourself', and then as you might imagine, that feeling of peace turned into dread. All of a sudden, I felt a force I cannot explain surround me. It was now around 7 am in the morning and I felt a strength that I knew, a strength that I recognised. I felt a love and strength from my father and my ex-husband that is very difficult to put into words. I felt their joint energies merge with mine, the power and determination welled up inside me. The spirit of my loved ones was pushing me forward. I showered, got dressed, opened the gates to the farm, filled the car with what we would need for our journey and I was ready to go.

My friend, who was quite an emotional woman, found herself in a real state of distress. "You can't do this, Lynn," she kept saying. "He will be ill, he will be upset." The voice in my head told me to tell her to be quiet; we were going and I didn't want to hear any negative emotions about it. She looked at me crying.

"Either you're with me or not," I told her, "but either way, my son is going to Anglesey today." She pulled herself together and went to her bedroom to get her camera and prepare for our journey.

There was no sadness or fear in my body. I felt positive and driven. It was now 10 am in the morning; the car was ready and so was I. I walked into Christopher's room and announced to him that he was to get up as today we would go to Anglesey. He took one look at me and put his head under his covers. "Don't Mum," he said. "I feel sick." The voice of his father was in my ear. 'Move him', he was saying. 'Today is the start of the rest of his life'.

I felt a strength come from my boots! I pulled the cover away from him and told Chris to get up. He started to panic, and then the voice within me shouted out as if I was possessed by my late husband. "Get up!" I shouted. "I don't care if you feel sick, we are going! Now get your bucket and your water and get in the car!"

I felt the strength of a thousand horses running through my body! Chris got out of bed. "I can't Mum," he said. "Please." Usually I would weaken as this was my son; my heart would be wretched out of my chest watching him suffer this way. But not today. I was not myself, that's for sure. I was stood there as two people, myself and my late husband. I felt his strength beside me and he wasn't taking no for an answer. Chris surprisingly grabbed his sunglasses and his headphones and got into the car.

My friend stood there in amazement. She pleaded with me to stop, not to do this. "Get in or get out of the way," I told her sternly. She climbed into the back seat of my car and I started the engine; my heart was beating out of my chest. I had done it, we were on the way.

FOURTEEN

The Journey to Freedom

That 100-mile journey was the quietest time I have ever spent in a car. Chris didn't even look at me and he was angry with me. He listened to his music and looked straight ahead. The familiar journey, which I had made so many times in my lifetime, went very quickly. We arrived on Anglesey to bright blue skies and warm sunshine. I felt a calm come over me; I had done it! What a feeling that was and we were 100 miles from the door that Christopher had been prisoner behind for many years.

I always get a feeling of love, a feeling of home, as I cross the Menai Bridge to our special island. Today was no different, I was home and my son was with me.

We headed on the road to Llygwy Beach, the place we had spent so many happy years with Chris and his father. We arrived to a very packed car park and in the summer months there is always a parking attendant on the entrance. As we passed the entrance,

Chris spoke up for the first time in two hours. "There's Alan," he said.

I looked at Chris and asked, "Where?"

"There," he replied, pointing to a man on foot just leaving the car park. I looked at Chris lovingly and told him that it wasn't his uncle, he was just wishing it was because it felt familiar to him.

"I know my uncle," he snapped at me. My friend told me to run after him and see if it was, while she went and bought a parking ticket.

I thought I would humour Chris and started out of the car park on foot after this man; I caught up with him and tapped him on the shoulder and to my surprise as he turned around I realised it was indeed my son's uncle! What a surprise I couldn't believe my eyes. "Oh my God!" I said to him. "What are you doing here? I have just arrived and I have Chris with me; it's the first time he has been out of the house in years!"

Chris's uncle just stared at me in amazement. "Do you still come fishing here?" I asked.

"No," he replied. "This is the first time I have been in three years; the last time I came it was to spread Ken's ashes," he told me.

"I can't believe you are here the same day as us!" Then to my surprise he told me how he was awoken with a shock at 4 am that morning. "I knew I had to come," he told me, "but I didn't know why."

He showed us where the ashes had been scattered and then my friend and I went for a walk and left Chris and his uncle to have a talk to reminisce about the good old days and their fishing trips with his dad. As I walked away, I saw my son's face in a different light. He was laughing and was so happy to be there in that beautiful place.

On my return, Chris told me that he wanted to go to the place where he sat for so many hours with his father. This was on the cliffs between Llygwy Beach and Moelfre the fishing town. Chris, my friend and I set out across the cliff walk towards the overhanging cliffs that he knew so well.

My friend was a budding photographer and she had brought along her camera. It was quite a walk to where Chris wanted to be so he ended up ahead of us while we oldies dragged behind. My friend's camera had a powerful lens. She stopped along the walk to take pictures of all sorts of things. As we turned a corner she called me back.

"Look," she said, "look at Chris – what is he doing?" I looked through the camera and there he was sat on the platform where he and his dad had spent so many happy hours together. He couldn't see us, but we could see him through the lens.

He had a huge smile on his face and looked as if he was talking with someone; he was happy. I felt all sorts of emotion welling up inside of my heart. He was free and like a caged bird, the spirit of his loving father and grandfather had set my son free.

As we caught up with Chris, he stood up and hugged me. Both of us at this time were feeling very emotional. "I love you Mum," he said, "and I couldn't have done this without you." The tears rolled down my face in complete happiness.

It was time to move from the rocks and go for a drink. It was mid-afternoon now and the sunshine was beating down on us. We started the walk back to the car park when Chris decided we would scramble down the rocks and walk back along the beautiful Llygwy Beach. My friend and I giggled. "How the heck are we getting down there," she said, "we are going to break our necks." We both laughed and held each other's hands to guide each other down.

Chris was ahead of us now and was in the distance walking along the beach and then all of a sudden, my friend said to me, "Who is that with Chris?" I could see a man and a woman but couldn't make them out clearly. Then he started hugging them. 'What on earth is going on', I thought! Chris didn't hug anyone but his nan and me.

What happened next was amazing! I reached the spot where Chris was standing and I was so shocked to see my old friend and her husband. Tracy was Michael's mum and Michael is the young boy who Chris was very good friends with most of his life. "Oh my God," I said out loud. "What are you two doing here?" We hadn't seen Tracy for many years.

"We are staying on the other side of the island," she told me. "We went to the paper shop this morning and there was a lady, an elderly lady who told us that the sunshine would be lovely on this beach today. So, we got in the car and drove over and we have been here all day."

Christopher was ecstatic; his uncle and very old friends all gathered on his favourite beach. We said our goodbyes and drove to the opposite side of the island to Rhosneigr. I couldn't visit our island without going to say hi to my dad, whose ashes were laid to rest in his favourite place not far from the airfield at RAF valley.

My son looked at me with such a loving glance. "Thanks Mum," he said, "for organising all of that."

"All of what," I asked?

"For getting everyone in one place for me today, important people who meant such a lot in my life."

"I didn't do anything," I told him. He looked at me and smiled, then as we pulled up in the car park of Ty Hen, I saw the most amazing thing. For a split second, I saw my lovely dad and my deceased husband stood on the hill.

My heart filled with love and emotion. None of this was a coincidence; Christopher's father and his beloved grandfather had indeed moved heaven and earth that special day, to bring us all together in one place.

We had been guided by spirit, all of us. The 4 am wake up call for me and Christopher's uncle, the old lady in the paper shop bringing Tracy over to the other side of the island; all of this had been orchestrated by the spirit of our loved ones. On hearing my plea for help, they delivered in a way that usually only happens in the movies.

My son had been delivered back to me and this day was to be a true awakening for both of us.

Christopher's story continues to grow, as does his strength. The drive home was not as quiet as the drive there; it was filled with light and love. Chris was not out of the woods yet, but by God's hand, was certainly pointed in the right direction.

It was this awakening that had a profound effect on both my son and me; there was no turning back now the spirits had found their way in and my life would never be the same again.

FIFTEEN

Ella's Ghost

My son David is engaged to a girl called Ellie; they soon set up home close by to her mum. It wasn't long after a wonderful holiday to one of my favourite places, Cyprus, until they announced that Ellie was expecting. They moved into a little house on the corner of a very popular street in Wallasey on the Wirral. Ellie's pregnancy went really slowly, I felt, and it didn't help that their little bundle of joy was to be two weeks late!

Ellie worked hard while she was carrying Ella as she was a waitress in a popular restaurant nearby. We put together a surprise baby shower at my house for Ellie and during the day we all had the chance to predict the baby's date of birth and weight. If I remember rightly, Ella was due around the 21April, however it was my birthday on the 5May and I just felt overwhelmed with the thought of her being born on my birthday. I remember Ellie and Dave saying they hoped it wasn't that late, with shocked looks on their faces.

Well, time went on and still no baby. After a trip to the hospital a few days before my birthday, the midwives decided that Ellie was to be induced, as she was now two weeks overdue. She was taken into hospital on the day before my birthday. It was a long day and the midwives told David that she wouldn't be born that day, things were taking longer than they thought. Ellie was exhausted but doing well, David told me.

My husband Ray had booked a table for us locally to celebrate my birthday, so we headed out to the restaurant keeping my mobile phone close by. I was so excited and anxiously awaiting any news; this little one was to be my third grandchild. Each one very precious to me, each one very different, Joe being the oldest, then Brogan who had only been born three months before Ella in February; I truly was a blessed lady to have such beautiful little grandchildren in my life.

It's funny but sitting here writing this chapter of my book, I now have been blessed with two more! My daughter Nicky has had a little boy who is a delight to be around. She called him Jade and Ella has a little sister Holly who is a massive character and never fails to make me smile. To say my cup overruns with the love from these children is so true, as my heart beats faster every time I think of all the blessings in my life, and I thank God every day for my family and for keeping my family safe.

Ray and I had finished our meal and I had phoned David before I went into the restaurant. He had told us nothing was happening and we were to continue our evening into Liverpool to meet with my sister Cath and her hubby, as we had made plans to go to the pubs to celebrate my birthday. We bought our tickets at the station in New Brighton. As the train was about to pull out of the station, my phone buzzed, and there she was born on the 5th May 2012. Ella Sophia, our little gift from God. I nearly exploded on the train. 'Mum and baby doing fine'. I was about to get off so we could go visit, but David said Ellie was exhausted and I was to come tomorrow. So, we left for Liverpool to celebrate the arrival of our new baby granddaughter.

All this excitement was another of those 'always listen to your voices' moments. I knew she would come on my birthday – something or someone kept telling me. These feelings I had back then and all through my life are the reason why spirits have now placed me at this computer writing this book. Everyone is capable of knowing – and I mean everyone. It's not just a gift given to some and not others; it's within every one of us and sometimes we just don't listen. I hope my experiences lead you to delve into your own physic mind and live your life how you are meant to. Once you listen, things come so much easier and life becomes that little bit sweeter.

Our visit to the hospital the next day was very exciting, until we arrived and I took one look at Ellie and realised she wasn't doing very well. The baby was fine but Ellie had lost a lot of blood, pints and pints to be exact. She was just sitting up in bed with a vacant look on her face. David told me she had not had a good time. It was a very stressful birth and Ellie would have to stay in hospital for a few days.

I felt her treatment there was appalling and it took

them days to realise that she would need blood transfusions before she would recover from the birth. Voices in my head where telling me she was in danger and I was to push for some help. Of course, the nurses didn't listen to me, but David did and he continued to fight Ellie's corner so that she could get the help she deserved.

For a whole week, David stayed by Ellie's side in the hospital to look after Ella. Ellie just wasn't capable of doing much at all; to be honest I was so glad when they were all able to come home, as there were a few times during the first few days that the feelings I was getting over Ellie were not good feelings. I truly felt at one point if they didn't move themselves in that hospital, that we could lose her!

The minute I saw Ella, my heart skipped a beat. I felt an instant connection to this tiny little girl. It was as if the angels had put an invisible cord attaching us both for life and I knew at that moment that life was going to be very different from here on in. Ella has a true spiritual gift that I will help her to develop over her lifetime.

Thanks to God and the angels, everyone was fine. Our prayers were answered and the day came when I arrived at the doors of the hospital to pick up my son and his lovely family. As I waited outside the hospital, I had this overwhelming feeling that all would be well and I was not to worry, my angels where reassuring me the whole time I sat waiting. I felt a familiar presence around me. This brought me comfort as I knew it was my dad. All would be well as he was here looking over his family.

The house that they lived in for a while was not ideal. It was damp and the landlord wanted nothing much to do with the repairs. There was black on the walls and everyone always seemed to be ill all the time. As I say continuously, *nothing is a coincidence*. We are all being guided by God on our journey, sometimes we take a wrong turning, but he will always correct our path eventually.

One day David and Ellie had been to visit Sue, Ellie's mum. She lived in the same street and had done for many years; it was this street where Ellie and her siblings grew up. The funny thing is that this was also the street where my mother had grown up; the world sometimes seems such a small place. There are reasons we all seem to stay where we are meant to be, as chapters of our lives actually link together when you look at the big picture.

David was so fed up of the damp in their little house that they had thought of moving. Ellie wanted to stay close to her mum so this was proving a problem finding something else to move to. As they left her mum's house they saw people moving out of a house over the road. David crossed the road and asked if the house was becoming vacant. They replied yes, and the man he was talking to was the owner of the house.

"We are looking," David told the man and he explained the situation up the road with the damp.

"It's yours if you want it," the man told David. "I know your mother-in-law and I am happy to rent my property to you and your family."

So, my son and his family moved into a bigger house, just up the street a little and it had such a lovely feeling to it. By the time they moved to this house, Ella was about 11 months old. She was such a gorgeous child – always smiling and her face always lit up as you spoke to her. She knew who was who and never failed to melt my heart every time I saw her. Even now, five years later, I always know that when I knock on that door this little girl is going to jump into my arms and hug me as if I have been away forever. Her love is pure and so very deep for such a little girl.

Although the house was bright and had a nice feel to it, there was always something that felt different at the top of the stairs. At this time, I was very much listening to spirits as I had opened my heart and let them come flooding back into my life. As I said earlier, Ellie was a waitress and my son David was the chef at the same restaurant, so I helped on a Sunday all day and evening to look after Ella whilst they both worked. I loved these Sundays and she was always such a good little girl to look after. I would pick her up around 11 am and take Ellie to work; Dave was already at work as he started very early. After dropping Ellie off, Ella and I would go straight to visit little nanny, my mum. The grandkids always called Mum 'little nanny' because she was about 4ft 5in, like a tiny little Welsh doll. I was 'big nanny' because I was taller…not because I was wider. (Just to set the picture straight in your head, ha ha).

We would then go back to my house and visit granddad. It's funny but Ella is nanny's girl. She always favoured me over her granddad; I don't know why, because he was lovely with her, but she always wanted me. Sometimes she would give in and play games with him but nanny's girl she was and still is to this day. We would spend the day at my house, have our Sunday roast, then we would head back to their house for Ella's bath and bed.

She was such a pleasure to look after. I only

remember her having one big paddy with me at my house and she had a real screaming fit! She threw herself on the floor in my bedroom and refused to move for an hour! So that's where I left her. She soon got over it and came into the living room where I was waiting for her. Nothing more was said and I have never had a minute's trouble from her since that day, and she is now nearly 5 years old.

As I had said in an earlier chapter, I was attending a spiritual development group by now and had been for around twelve months. We had spoken many times in group about something they called rescues. There are many occasions for whatever reason, the soul of a person does not go into the light and enter the safe haven of heaven. These souls then become trapped in our space and become what we know as ghosts. The thing is, the longer they are trapped here, the harder it becomes for them. It has been described to me by an earth-bound spirit as trying to battle their way through a deep fog. It is a struggle and not a very nice place to be, which I feel is why the spirits who are stuck here are angry and frighten those around them.

I used to visit David's every Thursday for my tea; it was nice to spend this time with the whole family, not just Ella, whilst mummy and daddy were at work. On this particular evening, David took me to one side and told me that Ella didn't want to sleep in her room. He told me that he would put her to bed and she would peep over her covers at the doorway behind him. One night he said to Ella, "What's wrong?"

"Daddy I don't like the shadow man," she said. As you can imagine, my son's face dropped.

"Who is the shadow man," he asked, "and where is he?"

Ella replied whilst peeping over her covers, "He frightens me, Daddy."

"Where is he, Ella," David asked.

"He is behind you," Ella replied. Well, to say my son nearly had a heart attack is an understatement. I knew straight away that this was the feeling at the top of the stairs. I had never done a rescue and wouldn't know where to start and I would be more worried about annoying them and making it worse for Ella. I told David I would speak to my friend who ran the group and ask for her help.

As soon as I arrived home that night I phoned her, she said she would help but that I was to go with her, as I had to learn sometime. We were to go and move them over into the light. This was not to be spoken about in David's house as the spirit would just hide when we arrived and we would not be able to help. I spoke to them both and asked that everyone leave the house on a certain day and that my friend and I would come alone and deal with this lost soul. I was frightened, I have to admit, as I had never done anything like this before. I picked up my friend and off we set to David's house.

When we arrived, the house was empty; David and Ellie had gone to the shops. As I put the key in the door, I felt very anxious. "It will be ok, Lynn," my friend assured me. We stepped into the hallway and straight away could sense a presence. We went upstairs to Ella's bedroom and we sat on the bed. All of a sudden the room went very cold. It was intense and quite spooky I have to say!

"Do you feel that?" Pat asked.

"Yes," I replied. "I do."

"It is a woman," Pat said. "She tells me that she lives here in this house." Pat told her that the little girl was frightened and that it was time for her to go. I sat there frozen and couldn't hear this spirit. "Why can't I hear her?" I asked.

"I don't know," replied Pat. "Try and connect to her."

As much as I tried, I couldn't hear her, although I could see her in my third eye. "I cannot leave," she told Pat. "I have lived here for many years."

"You are frightening the little girl," Pat told the spirit.

"Not me," the spirit replied. "I try to help, but he cannot help it, he is lost."

"Who is lost?" Pat asked, but right at that moment I felt a huge presence at my side. Another spirit had entered the room and was standing over me; it was a male and he felt very intimidating.

"Oh my God in heaven," I shouted. "Can you see him, Pat?" I asked very nervously.

"No," she replied. "I sense nothing apart from the lady." The lady told Pat that he was here, and he didn't want to speak to her, only me. I took a deep breath and asked him his name. He muttered something which I didn't understand. I was terrified – this was the first time I had spoken to an earth-bound spirit and I was frozen on the spot.

"He is sick," the lady told Pat, "and very difficult to deal with."

"I don't trust her," he said as he spoke to me. I reassured him everything would be ok; he continued to stand over me, which was very unnerving.

All of a sudden, my spirit guides came close. "Can

you help us?" I asked. "I don't seem to be able to communicate with this soul."

"He is ill Lynn," they told me. "In life he suffered with an illness called Alzheimer's. He did not believe in heaven because of this disease so he chose to stay in the street where he had died."

How very sad, I thought. "But he will be fine, it is part of his and your journey to show him the way home. He has waited for you for many years. Tell him if he stays here that he will be prone to the feelings and illnesses that affected him in life." My guides told me what to say.

I knew I had to help him, and suddenly I didn't feel afraid. Pat spoke to the lady and told her what we were going to do. "We are going to pass you into the light," she told her, "both of you. There are family waiting for you in the light."

"Wait," the lady replied, "there are more of us."

"More," Pat said, "where?"

"They are everywhere. They live between the houses in the street."

"Go get them," Pat told the spirit lady.

Within seconds, the room was full to busting! It was like being in a freezer, very intense; we were surrounded by lost souls. Pat took my hand and told me to see in my third eye the stairway to heaven with a doorway at the top. "See it open with the souls of everyone's loved ones waiting for these spirits."

We told them all to go to the light – their loved ones awaited them. What happened next I will never forget. It was something remarkable, as if from the closing scene in a movie. We asked the souls of everyone in the room to step onto the pathway and make their way to the light. Within an instant we saw the spirit of a child and several others shoot towards the doorway and disappear.

What an amazing experience that was. I felt very emotional but the room was still cold; the lady and the old man were still with us. I sighed and turned to Pat. "Oh no," I said, "they didn't go." All of a sudden, I heard, "Harry, Harry!" the old lady was shouting him. But he was too afraid to go. They stood on the pathway to heaven but Harry wouldn't move. He walked sort of funny, shuffling almost as if he couldn't walk.

"He is afraid. He won't go," said the lady.

"We are going to need help, Lynn," said Pat. The two of us called on the angels to help him to move.

Archangel Michael was the first to appear. "As a child," he said, "Harry loved to roller-skate. With this illness, their minds go back to their childhood. We must make this fun for him," said Michael and in an instant, roller-skates were on Harry's feet. The old lady held his hand with the angels on the other arm and they rolled him towards the open doorway of heaven. This was an amazing thing to see; Harry was still bent over and rickety but as they reached the doorway, I could see other souls awaiting his arrival. Within an instant, they had reached that bright light and Harry disappeared. The tears were rolling down my face; it was all so emotional. I could still see the doorway to heaven in front of me, and a shape standing in the doorway. It was the old lady. She smiled and waved and saying *thank you*, she stepped into the light and was gone.

I had never realised what this gift meant until that day. We helped many souls to cross over to their loved ones and my heart was filled with peace and love at knowing I had been a part of their transition. I found out from Ellie's mum Sue, that a lady called Jean had lived and died in Ellie's house and on describing the lady we saw, she was certain this was her. I often wonder if she has any relatives around. I would love to tell them the story of their mum or nan who stayed over this side to help out a neighbour whom she had known for years. As for Harry, he lived a few doors down. He had died more than 20 years previously; his family were one of the biggest on the Wirral and they ran the market gardens not far from where I now live.

Ella knew they had gone as she told Daddy that night. I knew from that day that Ella had a very strong gift that we must nurture and never let that gift die. Ella would tell me that she could see my 'gold'. I used to ask her what she meant; she would say, "Your head is gold nanny, you are an angel."

She would look at me with such love in her eyes. When I was suffering with high blood pressure one Sunday whilst Ella was with us in our home, we were sitting on the couch watching Disney. Ella looked up from the floor where she was playing, and she stared at me. Then she stood up and walked over. She sat on my lap with her legs astride mine facing me. She stared into my eyes and she put both her tiny hands on my face. She smiled and said, "Close your eyes, Nanny."

She placed one tiny hand on my forehead and one over my heart, then she started to chant: ber bum, ber bum, ber bum. I felt the love come from her heart to mine. I asked her, "What are you doing, Ella?"

And, to my amazement, she replied, "I am making you better, Nanny." She was 3 years old and already being guided by her angels and her guides.

Spirits told me never to let this fall away from Ella as she would be a very powerful healer one day. She would follow in nanny's footsteps.

She does suffer a lot with her tonsils at the moment but when I get the chance, I repay what she did for me that day. I say to her come sit with Nanny for a while whilst I do some magic on your tonsils. She does; she climbs on my knee and sits whilst I give her some Reiki. Then she will smile and say that's enough Nanny and climb down from my knee and get on with her day. It has got to the point now where I don't tell her I am doing this, I just send in the healing whilst she sits on my knee. She always knows, as she will say to me, "Are you giving me magic, Nanny?" and smile.

I am blessed that my grandchildren know about spirits and will always have a connection and always know that their nanny loves them beyond words in this life and the next.

SIXTEEN

Meeting Elizabeth

I always loved the early mornings, when everyone else was fast asleep and all was quiet and peaceful. There were no distractions, TV or radio, it was shear bliss.

One morning I was having trouble sleeping. It was still dark outside. I tossed and turned and in the end gave up and made my way to the kitchen. My two dogs lay fast asleep in their beds, and didn't even lift their heads to greet me. It was far too early for them; there was no chance these two would move for a few hours yet.

As always, in these quiet times of the day, my mind was filled with chatter. I made myself a cup of tea and made my way to my healing room, where I thought I would spend a couple of hours reading my book. This was short lived as someone was very excitingly telling me to look at the sunrise. Looking at its beauty, they had distracted me. The sun was rising from behind the lighthouse; it was a bright orange ball and with it came the promise of a beautiful day.

I was sitting in the perfect place; my healing room was filled with this orange light, everything felt so perfect. I could hear the birds singing away; they always seemed to be so very loud this time of day. I always imagined they were shouting, wake up, wake up, in their frantic little voices. The sun had risen quite a lot now and it was starting to blind me, as I was trying to read my book. I decided to move to the other end of the couch, and have the sun behind me to give me natural light to read by.

Around this time I was learning all I could about spirits, trying to make sense of all I had heard and was still hearing over the years. It was sometimes hit and miss if I heard them at all in a day. I realise now I was trying far too hard. These things are delicate and natural; it isn't something you can switch on and off as you please. I was still a little apprehensive if I saw spirits, or if something manifested in front of me. I have to admit, it really freaked me out!

I had been studying my Reiki as my guides wanted me to start to offer healing to my clients and I was now Reiki 2 and was booked in for my Reiki Master attunement very soon. Healing will be a very big part of your life, they would tell me. I already felt this in my heart, looking back now and writing this book I realise that I had seen spirits manifest themselves quite a lot over that summer. I think they were bringing me in slowly so not to frighten me. I have seen some miracles over this time and I know there are more to come. I will tell you about some of the healings in another chapter, as I have seen wonderful things happen that will take your breath away.

I just couldn't get into my book. I could feel spirits drawing near; I always felt them touch my hair, on my right side. It was an amazing feeling, the love you feel when you know they are with you. My little black cat Luna was driving me nuts, she wouldn't sit still and she was up and down off the couch, on the window ledge knocking everything over! 'Is there no peace', I said to her? All of a sudden, she jumped onto my healing bed and started to stare at the wall. She does make me laugh – she has more energy than me, that's for sure. I looked up, about to tell her *off* and to get down, when I saw what looked like a sparkling light on my wall, and this is what the cat was watching.

As I mentioned earlier, my animals are a big part of my connection to spirits and Luna is no exception, she has alerted me on many occasions since she moved into our home. I found her in my hay barn half starved, and I took her in and she has been here ever since. My guides tell me that she is my little familiar. A *familiar* is an animal that has been sent to you to help you with your work; these animals are very intelligent and know when spirit is about. They usually come and let you know when a spirit is trying to contact you and I know now that she was sent to help me to connect to spirits, and to make the journey an easy transition.

Many times, she has brought orbs into the room, which have driven her to distraction. I have video footage of these orbs. At the time, I had friends around for the evening; to their amazement when Luna came into the room so did all the orbs. I do know that some are flecks of dust as she was running around, but some of the orbs were huge blue in colour, and they changed direction as the cat chased them, as if they were playing with her.

One night when it was just my hubby and me, I

decided I would find out who these orbs were. An orb is a ball of energy given off by spirits. These beautiful flashes of light can be either a loved one or indeed an angel. On this evening I decided to ask questions.

"Who are you," I asked. They seemed to get brighter and brighter. The cat settled down as I started to question the bright blue lights. I asked first, "Is that you, Dad?" The orbs didn't move. I asked if it was Ken, my husband who passed over; nothing happened. Then we saw the room light up as I asked the question, "Are we in the presence of angels?"

Even my husband was amazed, although he told me not to show this video in public as he was in his PJs. We were in the presence of God's angels and they were playing with my cat! I do feel my little cat brings them in so not to frighten anyone. They see her first playing with spirits and it relaxes people. She truly is a magical cat and I don't know if I have told you but she is pure black, not a marking on her, and she has the most beautiful emerald eyes. She is very good luck for me and one of our family.

It is moments like these that I feel overwhelmed by the love I receive from all spirit forms.

This morning in the early sunshine was no different; my little cat had brought someone to meet me, as she brought my attention to the wall. I heard a voice say, "Hello Lynn." The voice was female and very faint. I looked up from my book and Luna had perched herself right on top of my healing bed. I was about to shout at her when she turned to face the wall again. She made me giggle sometimes, as it was almost as if she was saying, *look mum, a visitor*. She was watching the wall where the glistening light had been a few minutes ago. All of a sudden, the wall started to shimmer like diamonds before our eyes; the wall seemed to be moving; slowly a shape began to form on the wall.

I am not a Catholic girl, but indeed I am a Christian. The shape I could see seemed to look a little like the Virgin Mary with gowns over her head. Within seconds, the shape was there on the wall. I grabbed my mobile phone and took four pictures. These pictures have not turned out very well as the light in the room was quite dull but you can definitely see the shape of this lady, this beautiful shimmering being on my wall.

"I hope you are well, Lynn," she continued. "Today I want to introduce myself, and my name is Elizabeth." I stared at the wall in amazement.

"Hello," I replied. "Are you a new teacher?" I asked.

"In a way, yes," she answered in this beautiful voice. "I have come to help you with your healings," she said. "Hundreds of years ago, I too was just like you; I helped many people with many problems. I was a midwife, a doctor and a healer of all types. I would help the sick to heal, the grieving to find peace and to help them understand where their loved ones had gone when they passed over.

"I was exactly as you are, Lynn, people were drawn to me for my help; their spirit guides sent them to me. Myself and others worked tirelessly to help all we could and as you have found, sometimes our love and kindness was taken as a weakness. Those who were jealous of our gifts shunned us or took advantage of our love and our light. I know have found this Lynn, there are many you have trusted and thought as friends. These people have taken all they can, then leave you behind, sometimes wondering what on earth has gone wrong. It is their greed, Lynn, nothing more that makes them the way they are. Sometimes darkness gets in through the light. On most occasions, the person to whom the darkness penetrates wants the power the darkness promises, but you see Lynn all will end in tears. These people whom you thought were friends indeed were not. Their egos overtake the good inside them; heaven and God himself work on these people daily to try to make them realise what they are doing and he tries to lead them back to the light. These people do disguise themselves as light workers but their souls have a darkness which you do not have."

This was rather heavy for this time of the day, but I listened with great interest as I knew what she meant. This had happened to me, more than once.

"I know sometimes the removal of friends has been a painful one Lynn, but this must be done. God is protecting you as your work is important. Your friends will be filtered and those who shouldn't be in your life will go; those who truly love you will still be there even after hard times pass. Your energies are very special because you have no ego, you are what you are; this is how you have always been, you haven't changed, this is just simply you."

I listened in amazement. "You know me so well," I replied.

"Yes Lynn, I have known you all of your life – this one and many lives before. You are a beautiful soul and you always give so much of yourself for the good of others, and you give this so freely. Your qualities are many."

I felt myself blushing. "You are too kind," I replied.

"No Lynn, you are too kind and this is what brings the heartache. We are here now and we are guiding you; you will know who is who and where you are supposed to be. You have worked hard and now we will work together.

"I have much to teach you and I know that you are now ready to receive these teachings; great things will come from your work, you will see," she said.

"I am a very old soul, Lynn," she continued. "I am now your friend, you can call on me whenever you need me, and I have been sent to help you on your journey."

Within what seemed like seconds she was gone.

On my healing journey, I call upon the ascendant Reiki masters to help with my healings. I call upon the angels of healing and our lord Jesus. I didn't call upon Jesus at first as I felt unworthy of calling him to assist me, until the day he came without my asking, and spoke to me. "I am the healer of all healers, don't be afraid to call upon me for your healing work, I am everywhere I am all around you. I can be in many places at the same time and if with your clients is where I need to be, then I will come to you with just a thought to help you do your very best for these sick people." I cried the day Jesus came to me as I felt such love radiating from him.

After I have called upon Jesus, the angels of healing, the Reiki masters I call upon all light workers who come in love; this is when I feel Elizabeth draw close to me and rest her loving hand on my shoulder.

My clients have described a bright light to the right of them as I am healing; they describe this as if someone was shining a torch into their eyes. I have had many strange descriptions of things my clients have seen during their time here with me and these chapters are yet to be written.

I will share with you many healings that will make your heart miss a beat with the feeling of love from God and his workforce feeding directly into my clients.

Elizabeth has helped me with so many things over the past year; she has proved to be a wonderful friend and teacher and for this I am so very grateful.

SEVENTEEN

My Connection to Serene

Always having the enormous longing for my own horse, I feel is what brought me into a world which is very hard to explain, as spirits worked through the horses – every single one of them.

I took to the horse-world like pigs in muck. I loved the smell, the innocent look of trust they have when you shout their name, the whole picture: mud, rain, winter and summer. There is nothing like the bond between us. Serene was my fourth horse. Two had passed before her and one I had passed to my cousin, as I could see the connection between the two of them and I knew he would be loved and cared for beyond words. Those two were soul mates, I have no doubt of that.

Serene came to me as rather a lost soul and her owners didn't have much time for her, not because they didn't care but because the lady's daughter worked so hard and looked after so many horses. Some of these had been so neglected; everyone only has so many hours in a day and so as a very young horse she spent a lot of time alone. Many had looked at her but no one wanted to buy her. She was the wild card, the people of the horse world would walk by and not give a second glance. What a very pretty horse she was, chocolate brown in colour, a small white star on her forehead. She was a little tatty, as I said, she hadn't seen much attention. She was locked in a stable for long hours which caused her great upset and had been known to bring whole stable fronts tumbling down just to gain her freedom.

She came to me indirectly; my daughter Nicky wanted her desperately but we already had two others, Krakka and Major. We decided that Krakka could go and live with my cousin. We had a friend who stabled her horse on the same livery yard as we did. When she found out we were buying Serene, she had a fit and actually fell out with us for buying Serene. She said she was no good, and would always be a problem; I was letting my heart rule my head. Little did either of us know Serene was brought to me for lots of reasons.

In 2016 it was 20 years from when Serene became a member of our family. She is still here living with us and brings me love and peace every day of our lives.

The way things happen in life can sometimes remain a mystery but after the conversation I had a couple of weeks ago with my guardian angel it's now become apparent that Serene was indeed sent to me by an angel. I was sitting in the sunshine one beautiful May afternoon. The sun was warm and the sky was so clear. My house backed onto acres and acres of land covered with sheep, and we can see the Welsh hills from our windows. I loved to sit there early mornings and late afternoons and just watch the horses wandering around without a care in the world. I feel very blessed to live in such a wonderful home.

It's uncanny how the Angelic realm take these quiet opportunities to start their conversations with you. I was reading some research on my healing when an angel called my name. I have to say, even after all this time I still turn around to see who is there.

"What a beautiful day," she said to me. "You work too hard, Lynn and it's nice that you are out in the sunshine enjoying the first days of spring." My heart overflowed with the peace her voice brought to me. I told her of my love for this time of the year, and how the awakening of the earth in the springtime seems to also awaken me. I think it is something to do with me being a spring child as I was born in May and always loved to watch life breathed back into the land and the trees.

I am just as guilty as most people sometimes, even now, as I don't always hear my messages. I sometimes think straight past them and miss out completely. This is usually because I am busy or sometimes just trying too hard to hear what is being said to me.

I have always asked the guardian angel who has walked beside me my whole life, *what is your name* but most of my life, I didn't always wait for an answer. I have heard mediums and psychics saying that they hear their guides clearly, word for word. I would be lying if I said this was true for me as most of the time I feel they play with me. Sometimes the sounds I hear are a little strange, a little like what they call 'white noise'. It is hard to explain how I get my messages, however I will try. It's like watching TV and the story is shown to you piece by piece and like a jigsaw puzzle, you have to piece it all together in your mind then, hey presto, you have the story! It's not rocket science really, but my poor guides and angels sometimes must hang their heads wondering what the heck I am doing.

This day as any other, I felt my guardian angel draw close to me; she always brought me comfort by stroking my hair or touching my face very gently. The feeling on my face was just as if I had walked through an invisible cobweb.

"Hello," I smiled. "I know you are near." I heard her voice so clearly.

"Hello Lynn."

I have never thought to ask her if she had a name so I know that what happened this day wasn't coincidental and I now know she chose this time to teach me something on this lovely spring day. So, I asked my Guardian Angel, "What is your name?" I felt a sigh and also a giggle as she began to speak.

"Oh Lynn, if only you didn't run around with your head in the air, missing out on so much – you know my name already," she giggled to me.

"Do I?" I replied. "I don't remember," I joked with her.

"You do remember; it's a name that has been given to me for you to understand." I sat there baffled. "Our names are very long; they are shortened so you humans can remember them."

"Ok, so tell me." I heard a faint laugh. I do think my angel has a sense of humour; well she certainly did this day.

"You know my name, Lynn, think!" I was getting more and more frustrated.

"I will give you a clue. You have known my name

well for over 20 years now and spoke it every day."

"Really?" I said.

"Every day," she said. "This name is one you love. You have given it to projects and used it for other things. You spent many hours trying to gain my namesake back. We sent her to you but you parted with her when your daughter was ill. We sent you one with the same name so you could regain control of the situation, and you did. You were never meant to part with her Lynn, she is bonded to you for eternity."

I stared into space thinking this must be true. "Oh my God," I shouted! "Your name is Serene!" As I said this, the funniest thing happened. My lovely horse gave out a very loud whiney. I know this was my confirmation. I was correct. She gave a loud shriek of a whiney and looked straight at me. My husband Ray was in the doorway of our house.

"What was that in aid of?" he laughed.

My guardian angel seemed to jump with joy; she laughed and said, "Yes, it is! In the early years, I talked to you through her; she is of strong spirit and strong mind. She understands you perfectly and you her. We know of your love for her and your battle to keep her healthy. You hear her, don't you Lynn?"

"I do. I know when she needs me and she I; if ever I was stressed or sad, I would take myself to Serene and it would all flow quietly away. She has saved my sanity more than once over the years."

"What you didn't realise, Lynn, was that when you gave your troubles to Serene you were giving them to me."

This all made sense now. When my daughter was ill, going back some 13 years ago, I was struggling to cope with looking after the horse and my family. A friend of my sister's had visited from Yorkshire and had fallen in love with my lovely horse Serene. I decided after many tears and much deliberation that I would part with her, to this lady who promised to love her and look after her well. To tell you this was painful is an understatement. My heart was breaking the day I left the Wirral to travel to West Yorkshire with my girl in the horsebox. These were the years when I didn't listen to my voices or my angels. Everyone had been shut out for a long while. I thought it was my heart talking to me. 'Take her home, take her home, don't let her go, she isn't safe'. I thought this was me just panicking but of course it wasn't, and all would be revealed.

We dropped her off but didn't stay around; it was too painful. I explained a few things about Serene to the lady. Serene had always been a super star; she was a show jumper and also her dressage was lovely, not perfect but lovely. However, she was a typical thoroughbred. She spooked easily. I asked one last request, that she didn't take her out onto the roads until she was really used to her. The roads there were very narrow country lanes, with cars using them as cut through to avoid the busy main roads. When I look back, I can see that spirits were talking to me then, warning me that she wouldn't be safe if she stayed there. She promised she wouldn't and I said my goodbyes to my beautiful Serene and left, my heart in bits. I returned a few times to see how she was doing; she was well looked after and loved.

She had been there only six or seven months and never a day went by that I didn't pine for her; she would pop into my head in the weirdest of times. I think you can guess who was putting her there. I wasn't listening properly to what they were saying, as I had shut them out years before. My guardian angel must have been at the end of her tether with me. So, she very cleverly took a different approach. It was around this time, one lovely spring morning, my husband Ken was outside cleaning his motorbike, when an older lady asked him had we lost a cat.

"I don't think so," he said. "I am sure she was about this morning." She asked could she speak with his wife, so he came in and shouted me. On reaching the door, I was taken a little by surprise, as 15 years earlier I had met this lady. She was a medium; she was the lady who gave me my first reading. I always thought it was coincidence, that I received that reading that day 12 months after my father died in 1989, but now I know there are no such thing as coincidences – everything happens for a reason.

She didn't remember me, why would she? It's very hard to keep track of all your readings. I think it would drive you insane if you remembered every tear and every tragedy. Although one thing she did say to me was that she had been sent to my house that day and her guides told her I would be a big part of her life.

I asked her into the hallway of our home. I looked at her and in an instant it came to me. "Oh my word, you are Barbara the medium, I met you probably 15 years ago for a reading." She of course didn't remember but she talked about my house and my family and how beautiful I was, bless her. I asked her for some reason if she still did readings.

"I do," she replied, "but not as often now. Would you like to come for a reading she asked me" Without

171

hesitation I said yes, and after years of blocking the spirit world out, the doorway was flung wide open again and the world of the angels and my spirit guides seemed to flood straight back in. For this Barbara, my lovely friend, I would always be grateful.

I hadn't completely shut out my guides, it's just that their voices became faint amongst the hustle and bustle of my life. I just forgot to listen and didn't tune in to ask for help. We are all very guilty of this, I do believe this is why I have been asked to write this book, to awaken your guides within you, to help you to tune back in and learn to channel all that you hear. You see, the more people who are listening to their guides and guardian angels, the more light will be pouring into the world. With the wars and the people who have lost their way, if we pour light into the world, one day it will start to heal, one day the light will win the battle over the darkness.

I was excited with the thought of visiting Barbara for a reading; I hadn't been for so many years. It was a lovely day. It was May, the sun was shining and I felt so very happy. I got myself dressed in a pretty skirt and summer blouse; I had just had a birthday and as it was spring, my kids had bought me a lovely handbag which looked like an old fashioned straw bag, but on the side was one small apple blossom flower. I looked ever so girly. I strolled around to Barbara's house and she welcomed me inside. I was shown to a small room which I have to say was a little spooky! She had little dolls everywhere, which seemed to sit and look straight at you.

"Sit down," she said in her quiet little voice. She was such a lovely lady. She always looked glamorous with her black hair and beautiful face and she was heavenly to be around. She started my reading and was so very accurate with all she told me. Then in an instant she stopped and looked at me.

"I have the strangest thing," she said. "Lynn, do you have a horse in spirit?" she asked. Well, I nearly fell on the floor. Before I could reply, she said, "I see two eyes but they are different colours, one blue and one brown."

Years before I had lost my big boy Major. He was old and arthritic and had to be put to sleep. He was such a lovely horse. He was a huge shire cross to be exact. He had something they call a 'wall eye', one blue and one brown. I couldn't mistake the fact that this is who Barbara could see. I started to cry.

"He has come with an important message, Lynn," she continued. "Do not make the same mistake," she said. "She is not safe. You must go and get her and bring her home." I looked at her in complete shock! "He tells me you sold him to a lady who you thought would love him and treat him right, but she didn't and you have to go back and bring her home."

This was all too late for Major as she had left him out on the mountains of Wales and his arthritis had become much worse. I did however, buy him back and brought him home; he only lived for two years after he came home. I looked after him until the vets told me it was his time to go. Then I held his head whilst he was put to sleep humanely by injection. I had only had Serene two years when all this happened. I always thought that no horse could take his place but I was wrong, she didn't take his place but Serene took over where Major had left off. I had a massive connection to him also; God and the angels spoke to me through my animals – this was clear to see.

Barbara continued to talk about Major and his message for me. "You must bring her home; don't make the same mistake. If you leave her there, she will be in danger." My eyes welled up, then Barbara asked what this message meant from a horse. I said I didn't know, but deep down inside, I did. She asked Major what he meant, and then came a reply that blew my mind. "Serene by name, Serene by nature," Barbara told me and with the tears running down my face, I told Barbara what this all meant.

She listened to my words, then she replied, "You must go and get her straight away, something bad will happen if you don't. There is not a minute to waste."

My mind was upside down, I couldn't think straight. What was I to do; the lady who bought Serene would think I was losing my mind!

I went home in disarray. I told mum, who was living with me and my family at the time, what Barbara had told me. My husband Ken shook his head. "What the heck?" he said. "That's a load of rubbish."

Mum replied with, "I wouldn't be so sure; Barbara is very good at talking to spirit, I would check if Serene is ok."

Immediately, I got on the phone to my sister; she lived a couple of miles from the lady who had bought Serene. Janet told me not to worry that she had only just seen Serene the day before and that she was fine. I told Jan what I was told; I have to get her back. Janet told me that she doubted that the lady would give her back to me because she had grown extremely attached to her. I decided to drive to Yorkshire myself and visit Serene and her new owner.

The very next day I started out on my journey. The journey was 85 miles but I have to say I don't remember the majority of it. Spirits spoke to me most of the journey, or rather I thought it was just the noise in my head, until now as they remind me of this story. 'Do everything in your power to get her back, she is an important part of your future'. My mind was racing, 'what if she says no', I thought. Then I would hear the words again, 'Do everything in your power, you must get her back, we will help'. I remember thinking *who will help?* I really thought my dad was in that car with me that day, in fact I think he did the driving!

On arrival, I was taken straight to visit Serene. I cried as I was so desperate to see her again. She too was very pleased to see me; she let out a great big whinny. My heart skipped a beat as she came over to greet me. The connection was not broken; her love for me was eternal. I was so pleased to see she was in one piece. I went back to the lady's house and told her everything. She sat in amazement and told me that she always loved the mediums and that she would consider selling Serene back to me. She seemed to ponder on it for weeks and weeks. I was at my wit's end.

I texted her every day to check Serene was ok. She must have been fed up of me. Then one day she replied with the answer I wanted to hear. "You can have her back under one condition."

"Yes," I gasped. "You have to find me another horse that is just like her."

'Oh Lord', I thought. This was not going to be an easy task. Serene was very special as you now realise, and she was very talented. She jumped like a stag. I held my head up to the sky and asked God and my father to help me. I started to search the internet for the perfect horse, and would you believe I only went to visit one! In my search on the internet, I saw an advert for a horse that was in Aberystwyth in North Wales. This is where my lovely Serene had been born; 'this was a sign', I thought.

I have a dear friend, Anthony or Tony, as I call him. He lived on the property where Serene lived before I sold her. I rented a stable and field from him. He was really up for me going back for Serene, so when I asked him to accompany me to Aberystwyth, he jumped at the chance.

We set out early to visit the breeder and to see if this horse was suitable for the lady. We arrived after making good time; it's quite the drive from Wirral to Aberystwyth but the journey seemed to go very well. When we arrived in Wales, the guy who owned the farm greeted us. He asked us to walk with him towards the stable block. There she was, as large as life, a very large grey mare. We looked over her and checked she had no vices: biting, kicking etc, and she seemed perfect. She was bigger than Serene and I did worry that this would put the lady off, as she wasn't the most confident of people. Tony rode the horse for me and checked there was nothing wrong anywhere. She was lovely – seemed just perfect. I telephoned the lady and told her that this horse was just what she wanted. She agreed to come and visit her and we made the arrangement for that weekend.

It was I who had to pay for this horse, as it was my payment to have my beautiful Serene home at last. I was worried that she wouldn't like her. Panic was setting in. I turned to the breeder and shook his hand. "We will be back Saturday," I told him. As Tony and I walked away, my heart beating out of my chest, I turned and shouted back to the breeder, "What is her name?"

What he shouted back to me nearly knocked me over. "Her name is Serene." he shouted. I looked at Tony and we both gasped with amazement. Right at that moment I felt this wave of calm come over me, I felt the angels telling me all will be well. The panic was over.

You might be wondering why I am telling you this story of how I came to bring my beautiful horse home but she played a very big part of my spiritual awakening and we were never meant to spend life apart. The lady loved her new horse and I brought my special girl home, and she has never left my side again. She is 23 years old now and has had many ailments. It wasn't a car on the busy road in Yorkshire that would cause Serene to be ill, it was the rich grass on the Yorkshire dales that caused something that she would have to live with for the rest of her days.

I cannot imagine a day without Serene but the angels tell me she cannot live forever and her time is limited as her condition worsens year by year. I cannot see my beautiful soulmate in pain and I know she will not die of natural causes, her will is too strong. One day my dad will come to take her home, and I know she will be loved as much in heaven as she is here. On this day my heart will break in two but I know, as with my other animals, the day it's my turn to return home, there will be a line-up of animal souls waiting to greet me with my loved ones. This gives me great comfort; all is not lost, I will see them all again when my time here is done. As I sit here writing this, it is 8am in the morning on a very cold November day. I finish here as my girl stands patiently waiting for me to put on her warm rugs and turn her out into the field for the day with her friends. To say 'I love her dearly' just is not enough to paint the picture of our life together.

I dedicate this chapter to my lovely girl, forever patient, forever Serene.

EIGHTEEN

Our Guardian Angels

I have had many teachings from the angels and my spirit guides, and one I remember so very clearly is the answer to the question that I asked during a meditation. The question was, 'do we all have guardian angels at our sides'? On asking this question, I was prepared again for one of my many journeys, these journeys were full of knowledge and understanding.

Raoul took me by the hand and swept me once again to the beautiful place we all call heaven. As usual, the weather was perfect and the sky was the most beautiful deep blue.

I was taken to a place he called the nursery; this was just as it sounds. We stepped inside and to my amazement there were thousands and thousands of tiny souls all waiting patiently in an orderly queue. We walked down the line of brightly gleaming souls; at the end of the line was what looked like a checkout at the supermarket. Behind the checkouts were the brightest lights I have ever seen, they were so bright I could hardly look at them.

I asked Raoul, "What are those bright lights?"

"They are the guardian angels," he replied, "and each tiny soul is to be placed into the chosen family tree. There is a contract agreed upon between God and the tiny soul. This contract is their pathway in life. I know this sounds rather regimental," Raoul continued, "but everyone has their pathway agreed before they are born."

There are times in our lives when we feel we are meant to do something else, or things just are not going right for us. The road is rocky and the pathway is difficult. It's times like these our guardian angel steps in and tries to steer us in the right direction. Sometimes they are not successful and you continue along the wrong pathway. The guardian angels will continue to steer you to where you are meant to be and with some hard work on their behalf and the hope of God, you will arrive, exactly where you are meant to be.

We watched as these spirits received their contracts of life, then they were moved on to the next stage through the checkout, so to speak. "How are the guardian angels chosen for us," I asked.

"Watch and learn," said Raoul.

We stepped forward and stood to one side so we could watch the process. As each soul stepped forward, one by one you could see the lights dim down a little amongst the guardian angels. The soul was beckoned and as they stepped forward, the most magical thing happened. One of the guardian angels' lights would become so bright I just couldn't look at it; this is how they are chosen. Each guardian angel is destined for one of these souls in the room. As the soul steps forward, it ignites the love inside of the angel who will walk beside it until that soul one day is brought home to God.

What an amazing sight to see. I felt overwhelmed by the beautiful scene in front of me. "If everyone is given these amazing angels before they are conceived," I asked, "how come there are bad people in the world who do such terrible things to others?"

"That is a good question," Raoul answered. "Unfortunately humans are given also something called free will. The free will is a choice for the human, so he walks the path they want to, sometimes regardless of their guides and their angels. This is very sad but this is a gift that humans are also given at birth. Free will is very powerful; it can be used for good but can also be used for bad."

"This is known as the 'light and the dark', 'good and evil' – there are many names this is known by. We spend every minute of every day steering our humans towards the light, but in the world, for every light space in time there is a dark space. More often than not the light will conquer over the dark but there are unfortunately times when dark will win that battle."

'I don't like the sound of that', I thought. "Why can't God just sort everyone out?" I asked.

"It is more complicated," he replied. "The more light workers on Earth, the brighter the light becomes. This is our goal, to show many people the way of the light, and steer them away from the darkness. One day Lynn, this will happen and God's foot soldiers, the Archangels will have spread the light across the universe.

"Everyone works within the light from the moment of conception; the guardian angels are with them in the womb and through birth, and then on every step of their journey in life. The angels will step in and give a gentle push in the right direction to make your transition in life a smooth one.

"The small child will always know they are with their guardian angel, and small babies sometimes will look over the top of people's heads towards their crowns. They are taking a look at that person's angel. A newborn baby can communicate with spirit and its guardian angel. They can also see your guardian angel," he continued. "They see the bright light that walks besides us.

"Sometimes you will hear a grandmother or mother say: 'this child has been here before'. "A child has no hang-ups and no inhibitions; they just believe and they remember their life before they were born. They remember previous lives and what their guardian angels looks like, and the feel of their energy. Your angel will walk beside you until the day of your passing. On your deathbed you will see your guardian angel and they will take your soul from your body when that body has died. They will then sweep you up and take you home to God."

I was amazed by the beauty of what I was being told. "My guardian angel is quite playful," I told Raoul.

"You are a beautiful soul Lynn, and your guardian angel has guided you through your life safely. Sometimes they can be heard to laugh and sometimes you will hear the voice of your angel as clear as day. They love you, Lynn unconditionally, and will stand beside you through thick and thin. This is their job, to protect you and guide you.

"You have written in your book how your life has been blessed with the light, even though at times it may feel as if you were forsaken. Your guardian angel has always been at your side, even at times when you felt she wasn't. We have taught you how to ask for help when needed and now we want you to pass on this knowledge to all who read your book. Listen for the words as told to you in the story about your horse, look for the signs and teach everyone to do the same, in your classes or your writing. You will reach many and for each person you touch with your work, you will bring more light into the world.

"You have heard me tell you many times Lynn, you are just like a lighthouse, and your light can be seen for miles around and like a ship at sea, people will be brought safely back by your beautiful bright belief. Continue on this pathway, this is your divine purpose. Now it's your turn to help others realise theirs.

"Remember Lynn we are here beside you on every step of your journey."

NINETEEN

The Caverns of Knowledge

During the summer of 2016 I would spend many an early morning sitting in the garden just enjoying the horses and the smell of the summer air. On this particular morning, I was sitting on my swing in the garden; the birds were singing, my dogs were at my feet and all was just so peaceful.

I could see my beautiful horse Serene grazing in the field without a care in the world. How lucky I was to live in such a tranquil place. We have barns and stables on the property and in the spring, the swallows would migrate and nest in our stables. It was such a lovely feeling to see the first swallow arrive all the way from Africa; how clever they were, I thought. It was fabulous to see the nests repaired and the new babies hatch, only to make the long journey home in the autumn. Nature is such a beautiful gift from God and I think that the more you enjoy it, the closer to God we become.

My guides and the angels would take this chance

to come and talk with me – this one particular morning my guide Raoul came to be with me in the beautiful sunshine.

"Good morning Lynn," I heard a voice say.

"Good morning Raoul," I replied. It's funny because my guides always chat to me as if they were human. I do think this is so that we connect to them more easily. Raoul is I believe one of God's foot soldiers. The angels are His teachers, calling on us all around the globe to help us realise many things. Raoul was dressed head to toe in white robes; the white of his clothes was blinding. His eyes gleamed like the sparkling sea. He looked as a man of his sixties would…a white close shaven beard, white hair and a handsome face. I know they give this appearance just for our benefit, to make us feel comfortable and safe.

"I have come to take you on a beautiful journey." Raoul smiled as he said to me, "I have many things to teach you Lynn, today and I would like to give you some more knowledge of heaven."

I was very excited, as I know my journeys are always filled with a greater knowing and understanding. "What do you want me to do?" I asked Raoul.

He said, "I am going to show you today where all inventions and inspiration comes from. As you know Lynn, there is no such thing as coincidence, everything ever invented, every inspiration known to man has been put there by spirit. The little seed of thought then turns into a masterpiece; it's all very simple when you know how!" he laughed.

"The wheel, the light bulb, cars, planes, trains," he smiled, "this list is endless. Once the idea is placed by us, we have to keep reminding the host, and by tapping away at their imagination, eventually they remember, and they bring those inventions to life.

"There are different realms of existence in the place you call heaven Lynn, but you do realise that heaven is just another area of space; it is not miles up into the stars, it is just one reach above your crown. Spirits work daily to help everyone to be the best they can possibly be. These spirits work to help your life here on earth; we strive for good and for opportunity for all humans. Sometimes they will stray from their given pathways but ninety per cent of the time we can bring them back to their life's purpose. You are born with a certain pathway, but the thing we all love about the human nature is of course, CHOICE. You are given the choice but most of the time, if you choose to take a different pathway to what you were destined, you will always be guided back to your given pathways later in life."

Raoul hardly stopped for breath, as I sat there in the lovely sunshine; a thought ran through my head, 'how on earth will I remember all this information'? I have a head like a sieve! Straight away, Raoul smiled at me, because of course he had heard my thoughts.

"Do not worry Lynn," he said, "you will not forget. I have been assigned to you, I am your guide for your book."

I gasped! "My book?" I said. "Dear Lord, what were you thinking! My grammar is awful and my spelling is worse! And what would I say? my With my memory, well a book would take a million years to write."

Raoul laughed, "We will give you the confidence Lynn, and we will also jog your memory.

"What will I write about?" I asked.

"You will write about everything you know, and beyond. Along with the angels who guide you and your team of spirit teachers we will help this to flow, you will be surprised."

"You are not kidding," I laughed. "I will be surprised!"

"This is your life's purpose Lynn; we need others just like you to realise that they can also connect to spirit. When others read your work, they will come to realise that they too have had similar experiences, and they will start to act on this, therefore bringing a new light to the world. Light will always win over dark but it doesn't stop the souls who have given up to the dark to keep on trying. If we fill the world with light we will blind the dark and fill each corner with a strong and powerful energy and dark will not be able to exist there.

"This is a part of your journey Lynn, now quiet and listen to what I have to tell you, or the day will pass by and we will not get to visit the caverns of knowledge. I want you to understand about the mechanics of these outer realms and how God puts everything in place with his light workers and keepers of knowledge. You will learn why people are chosen to be the host, into which we place the seed of knowledge and from where these inventions and magnificent ideas come from. I am going to take you on a journey, I will show you things that will amaze you."

I was glowing with excitement. "You must come with an open mind Lynn," said Raoul. "There is a great deal for me to show you; are you ready?" he asked me.

"Yes," I replied.

"So then, close your eyes." And in an instant, I felt Raoul take my hand. It's hard to explain the feeling when you are touched by spirit, but I will try; it's like the butterflies in your stomach when you are on a fairground ride or the soft touch of a tiny child. It's comforting and beautiful and it can be very gentle and very faint. You could miss that touch if you were not used to it, but once you realise what this is you are sensing it lifts your heart every time it happens to you. When a loved one comes to visit them sometimes they will touch your hair very gently, or you feel something on your face, a bit like you have walked through an invisible web. It is all very subtle but once you feel it, you will never mistake it again. It brings you great comfort to know your loved ones, your guides and the angels are nearby watching over us.

Within what seemed like seconds we had arrived at the most beautiful place, the sky was so blue. Everything around me was like all four seasons rolled into one. I have always been a lover of the four seasons, the stunning reds and oranges of the autumn, the sparkly white frost and watery sunshine of the winter, and the lazy summer days which seem to go on forever. Most of all I love spring; everything always looks dead after a long winter, the trees are bare and the shrubs are dull but then all of a sudden it's as if life has been breathed back into everything around us. It overwhelms me when the apple and cherry blossom burst out and the air is filled with a beautiful fragrance. Imagine opening your eyes and seeing all this rolled out into one explosion of colour, it was amazing to say the least. The air was so fresh and clean; it was a beautiful summer's day. Raoul looked at me and told me that we can only stay for a little while. "We have a great deal to see, are you ready Lynn?" he smiled.

"I am, I replied, but I have a question."

"Go ahead," said Raoul.

"Well you see, I thought spirit would be everywhere and there is not a soul in sight, where is everyone?"

"Ah," he said. "They are here but you cannot see them; just for today they are hidden from view."

"That doesn't seem fair," I said with a frown.

"They would be too distracting for you, Lynn. I know you have loved ones in heaven, but we have work to do and I know you Lynn, you wouldn't be concentrating if you were surrounded by your loved ones."

I did feel quite sad at the thought of being brought to heaven but not getting to say hello to all those I love and miss so very dearly.

"Please don't be disappointed," Raoul said with such a beautiful smile. "Come on let's get a move on," Raoul had one of those faces you couldn't stay mad with for long. "Lynn, all will be revealed in time." We stepped forward as if through a silky veil, and in front of us stood a building like no other I have ever seen. It was enormous. There were green lawns on either side of the pathway on which we were walking. The path was as straight as a pencil; the front of the building was breath-taking with great big white marble pillars which seemed to gleam and glisten like crystals.

There were two colossal statues standing either side of the doorway which I was told were made of pure gold. What an extraordinary sight this all was. As we walked up to the doorway, the double doors opened. The light from inside seemed to spill out like liquid. I can imagine the look on my face of pure amazement.

"This is the museum Lynn," said Raoul and we stepped inside into the light of this wonderful building. "Everything that has ever been invented is in this museum, everything," he smiled.

Gosh, this building must be bigger than I thought. It felt as if we had been in there for hours. Looking at everything was very interesting; some of the inventions were so very simple and some so very important to the world. He continued with my tour and told me how these inventions came about; I frowned and told Raoul that the world would be a better place without some of the things in this room. But as always Raoul had an answer. "Yes he told me, you are probably right, however the world must evolve – it cannot stand still."

We looked at everything ever invented. Some I cannot even remember: the wheel, electric lights, cars, buses, farm machinery…I could go on forever. Still, I noticed there was not a soul in sight.

"It's nearly time to return Lynn, but before we go I have one last thing to show you."

'Wow, there is more', I thought!

Before us were a large set of silver gates. As we walked towards them, I heard a clunk; the gates opened slowly and Raoul turned to me and smiled. "This is the field of aviation," he said. We had stepped through the gates into the open air. It was amazing looking at all the aircraft, hot air balloons and everything that has ever flown was on this air field. They were all lined up as if awaiting take off orders.

"Wow," I gasped in surprise, "what an amazing place." Straight away, my childhood came flooding back. I remembered when I was a little girl my dad would take us to Liverpool airport. Mum would make us a picnic and we would sit and watch the planes landing and taking off for hours. "My dad would love this, do you know has he ever been here?"

"Indeed he has," replied Raoul, "and this is one of your father's favourite places." I felt a little sad knowing that my dad had been here, but I couldn't see him.

There were a row of fighter jets up in front of me, just like the ones in RAF valley on Anglesey. I explained about Mum and Dad's caravan near the RAF base and how Dad would sit for hours with his binoculars watching the fighter jets take off and land during training. When my dad passed some 28 years ago now, we took his ashes and scattered them near the base. We felt this is where he would want to rest, in his favourite place.

Everywhere was so bright, the sky was clear and blue and I truly was in heaven. Raoul put his hand on my shoulder. "It's nearly time to leave, Lynn," he said to me in such a gentle voice. I looked at him with tears in my eyes. "But before we go, I have something for you; you have worked so hard and studied everything we have shown you. Without hesitation, you have put your faith in us. So, for this I have a gift for you." He pointed towards the fighter jets; the light behind them was so much brighter than everywhere else. Raoul gave me a slight push towards this light. I looked at him and he said, "For you Lynn," then he stepped away from me.

I saw a shape come from the side of the jet planes,

a tall figure in full RAF uniform. I felt my heart beat hard in my chest; I could not believe my eyes, I had so many emotions running through my head. I recognised the shape of this person…could it be? I gasped, then I saw his face. He glowed like an angel, it was my dad. I ran towards him, tears running down my face. He had the biggest smile I have ever seen. I flung my arms around him, he felt as we do: solid, a person, my dad.

"Lynn," he said, "I told you I was ok, I have missed you so much, I have been watching you all for many years, although there is no time here so it doesn't seem long since I left you all." We talked and talked for what seemed like hours. He told me how he watches all his family and tries to guide them daily. "Sometimes to no avail," he laughed. "I just love the grandkids and great grandkids, how they are so open to spirit, how they laugh and have no hang ups on having a full-blown conversation with me," he laughed. "I have helped with homework more than once," he smiled.

"I know you have been upset that you don't always hear me, Lynn, but there are reasons for this, as I know you have been told but I am always around you and all the family. When you call me I am there. It makes me smile how you will say to me, 'show me you're here, Dad', and you have the angels literality moving heaven and earth to give you the sign you ask for. A two-man light aircraft, you don't see many over your house do you Lynn," he laughed, "except when you ask for a sign.

"I have things I want to say to you Lynn, I want to thank you from the bottom of my heart, for the promise you made to me when I was so terribly ill in hospital."

"I remember, Dad," I replied.

"I was so worried about Mum, I asked that you always watched over her, never leave her lonely and to pull her in closely. You kept your promise without hesitation, every holiday for many years Mum was counted in, every Christmas dinner and every doctor's appointment and hospital appointment you have never let Mum down. I know there were times Mum was so very ill and you and Ken took her into your home. I remember this room was to be for David when you first thought of it, but when Mum was so ill, David offered his room to her. He will remember," he laughed, "the night I came and thanked him for what he had given to Nan. He was with his girlfriend; they both saw me and felt me sitting on the end of the bed. I think that memory is something she won't forget in a hurry," he laughed again.

"Your love has made Mum's life a full one. You have all had a hand in Mum's life, you have all pulled together as a family, and everyone has always done their best, and for this I am truly grateful.

"There were many times you thought you would lose Mum, as she has fought some terrible illness in her years but it wasn't her time, Lynn. She was meant to oversee her family for many years and this she certainly has done. Make the most of her as I know you all joke and say she will live forever, but she won't; she is 82 years old now and she has the constitution of an ox but her day will come, as everyone's eventually does. I will wait for her until the day it is time and I will bring her home to be with me and other loved ones who have passed before her and there have been many. I have prepared a cottage on our beautiful island looking over the sea; Mum has always said she would like to look out to sea one day from her window. This is what we will have. Until that day know that. Mum knows all you have done for her through the years, she knows everything and she loves you with her whole heart, as do I."

I felt Raoul touch my shoulder. "It's time to return home," he said.

"Please no," I answered with tears in my eyes. "Let me stay just a while longer. I have so much to tell him."

"I hear your thoughts, Lynn," Dad replied. "I hear you every day and I am proud of your work. Don't let anyone tell you it's nonsense as you are very special and are bringing love and peace to many people. They have given both of us a gift Lynn; from now on you will hear me often. I am to help you with your writing. I am always near you and all the family. I do spend a lot of time with Mum and I do believe that sometimes she knows that I am there. You will be allowed to visit me again; now go home and enjoy your family and your life, be happy in knowing I am here and always will be."

Dad hugged me tightly, and in that instant, I was home, back in the sunshine in my garden. All was very quiet. There was not a sound, and then all of a sudden, the sound I always asked for, a humming from over the sea. I looked up into the sky just in time to see a light aircraft fly over.

My dad was near and I felt peace knowing that he would always be close by.

TWENTY

When God Takes You Home

It was 2016 and it had been years since I had seen my old friend Barbara. There were times I would think about her and wonder how she was. She would telephone me sometimes just for a chat but not very often. More often than not, I would hear her call me. I would feel her energies around me and I just knew that she was wanting me to contact her and when I asked her, she would tell me that she had sent her guide to fetch me and this time was no different.

Ray and I were just getting ready to go on holiday, when I heard a voice say, "Lynn, Lynn, Barbara needs you."

I picked up the phone and called her number. Her husband answered the phone and said Barbara isn't very well. He told me she would love to see me. I got myself ready and headed to their house. I was so surprised when I saw her and she looked so tiny in her bed.

"Lynn, I have been calling you, I have missed you

so much. I am so ill," she told me, "and I am in terrible pain." I offered her some healing which she gratefully accepted. "I have missed you dearly," she told me.

"And I, you," I replied.

"I have spoken with my guide, she is a nun. She nurses me and holds my head on her lap. They have been telling me about you and I am so pleased that you have decided to give in to the voices in your head; they will guide you well. I don't have long now," she told me. "I am gravely ill and I am surrounded by my family. They have come to take me home." This made me feel so very sad, hearing these words from a dear old friend.

"I have been calling your name, and as always your heard me. When it is time for us to leave here and return home, our gifts will pass to another. I give my gift to you. I have loved you like the daughter I never had. Take care of your gift and always do your best for everyone, but remember that you too are important. Don't wear yourself out."

This was good advice from my dear friend. I told her to lie back and close her eyes, and I called in the angels and the healers and asked them to bring peace to this lovely lady, who had served them for many years. The room was filled with spirit and the love for my friend was glowing all around us. I told her that Ray and I were going away on holiday and we would be back in a week. "As soon as I return, I will come and visit."

She smiled and gave me a kiss on the cheek, "Lots of love to you Lynn," she said as I walked away. "You have a lovely holiday."

The holiday seemed to go very quickly and we

returned home on the Wednesday afternoon. I had a full diary for the Wednesday night and planned to call Barbara in the morning.

It was 6 pm in evening, and my client arrived excited about his reading. The reading went well except for one thing, I kept seeing the face of my lovely friend Barbara. I felt her presence, which wasn't unusual for her as she was capable of sending her spirit to me if she needed me over the years. But this felt different. I always knew Barbara's spirit but this time she was chatting to me, not very clearly but nevertheless, I could hear her voice.

I did apologise to my client as at first, I thought this voice I could hear was for him. The reading went well and my client was very happy with the contact he had made with his mother who had passed just recently.

After my client left, I telephoned Barbara's house to check she was ok but there was no answer. I did a drive by in my car to see if there was anyone home but there were no lights on nor a car in the driveway. I went back home after pushing a note through the door and waited for her husband to come back to me.

The very next day my daughter Nicky called and asked would I run her to B&Q. I told her I would come and pick her up in half hour. We headed to the shops and we were in the aisle when I heard my phone message ding. I opened my phone and it was a message from Cath, my sister. I felt my heart skip a beat as I read this message. It read, "Hi Lynn, do you know a local medium from Moreton?" Straight away I knew, she was talking about Barbara. I replied, 'YES, why'?

"I am sorry but she has died," was the message I

had returned by my sister.

Nicky came around the corner to me in tears. "What on earth is wrong," she asked me.

"Oh my God," I said, "she is dead."

"Who is dead mum?" Nicky looked at me wondering what had happened.

"It's Barbara," I cried. "She has died. Cath just texted me." I felt so very sad at this news but also I felt relief as my dear friend looked so poorly when I visited the week before. I texted Cath back and asked, "When did she die?" Then came the reply that made me understand what had happened the night before.

"She died at 5.30 last night," Cath replied.

When my client was having his reading, Barbara had just passed. She had come to say her goodbyes to me. I felt very touched by this experience. It's been nearly 12 months now and Barbara comes to me on a regular basis. In fact I visited a medium myself not so long ago as I wanted to hear from someone else about things that were going on in my own life. Barbara was one of the first to come through to talk with us. She stood by my shoulder and spoke to this medium about me. It was quite funny as I had never met this lady before, but Barbara told her straight away, "Don't be fooled by her you know, she doesn't need you, she doesn't need anyone's help, she just needs some confidence that's all," she told this lady. I smiled and took in everything that this lovely medium was telling me.

You would think after 60 years of bringing comfort to others that Barbara would have taken time out now and left the spiritual guidance to others, but no, she hasn't. She is there for most of my readings helping me to bring love and peace to whoever is sat on my couch.

I know that sometimes, in fact most of the time, it is very sad when someone you know or love passes over but what we have to remember is what I tell my clients day in day out; they are not dead and they have just finished their time here on this earth. They will continue to live on in this place we call heaven still having a full existence but without the earthly structure we call our bodies. It is the body that dies but the soul of everyone and every living thing, will live on forever.

There are many vast planes in heaven and much to do; my dad once told me that he can travel the world in a day. He just has to think of where he wants to go, and then he is there.

Your spirit is free and can be sometimes in many places at once; there are no limits as we have here, you will be as free as a bird and as light as a feather.

What wonderful thoughts to take with us into our later years here on earth.

TWENTY-ONE

The Author and the Medium

I have a very dear friend her name is Bev; she has been one of my biggest supporters for this book from day one. She has encouraged me every step of the way and helped me even when her workload is full. She reads every chapter and edits my terrible spelling and grammar. What a superstar and I know she will be smiling when I say the Maldives here we come; when this book sells, I will take her for a long holiday, and Beverly you can take that to the bank, my lovely friend.

We have had many holidays to her house in Abersoch, North Wales and we have had many spiritual experiences whilst being there. I remember the time it was early summer 2016 and we had gone to her holiday home for a long weekend. We had walked the dog on the beautiful beach and headed home to make some tea and of course and to open a nice bottle of red wine. We were both tired from the journey so we decided we would sit and watch a film.

"This is fabulous," she said to me. "It's called The Labyrinth and it's right up your street," she smiled. We sat down with the dog at our feet, and started to watch. Bev was right, it was an amazing film but not without interruption! My spirit guides and our loved ones had filled the room. It was quite funny; every time a different scene came on I heard a voice telling me the outcome. I started to repeat to Bev what was being said to me. We both thought it was hilarious but I was a little cross at them as they were ruining my film. All I could hear was their giggles as they continued to reel out the story to me; I was clearly being teased and they all found it very amusing.

Before we knew it, the film was over, but spirits remained. They talked to us about the film and the Knights Templar. They talked about a trip Bev and I had taken to France, where we stayed in an 800-year-old chateau. This place was indeed the most haunted house I have ever stayed in. The house was heavy with spirits who were stuck in time, all of them trying to communicate with us; the feeling was of great sadness in this house. I could see ordinary people and knights. There were ladies dressed from head to toe in grey uniforms, the likes of which the servants would have worn many years ago, and I could see others dressed in finery and then of course the knights in their armour. It was quite an experience. Bev was amazed as she too could feel all these spirits around us. We were both quite chilled at the whole thing. I won't pretend, there was such a lot of history within those walls of that very grand chateau and I imagine many stories that could have been told. This film we had just watched reminded me so much of that visit we made to France that year.

Bev and I were chatting about all sorts of things and spirits were helping the evening along nicely. She had visits from some family members who had passed over and I was able to give messages to Bev from these people. The whole weekend was clearly meant to be, as we were both visited by our loved ones. But, after a couple of bottles of wine we decided to give in and go to bed. I slept like a log; I was exhausted. I awoke in the morning to the sound of Bev on her phone; I went down stairs as my morning cuppa was calling me.

I made us both a cup of tea and sat down at the breakfast table. "What's wrong with Megan?" I asked. Megan is Bev's beautiful golden Labrador.

"I don't know," Bev replied. "She had been strange all morning." Then I heard the whisper of spirits.

"Oops," I said to Bev. "I think our visitors from last night are still here!" The poor dog was demented. I don't think she had slept a wink all night. I wanted to show Bev the spirits as sometimes they will show up on a video or a photograph. I filmed the room and they never let me down – the room was filled with orbs. We got a picture of a streak of light shooting across Megan. Megan was not amused, so I asked spirits to leave. They had stayed for an all-night party, and now it was time to go!

I can't remember why we got onto the conversation of Bev's friend Pen, but we did. Bev told me about her and she had also told Pen about me. Pen loved the whole concept of mediums and spiritual things and said to Bev she would love to meet me. Bev told me that Pen was also writing a book. She had never written anything before but this book just started to come to her, and she loved every minute of it all. I agreed that one day when I went to visit Bev we could get together and have a visit; this never seemed to come about as the months passed and all of us were busy people.

I continued to sit and write as spirits had instructed, but when writing, this lady's face would come to me, and my spirit team would say, "Lynn you must visit." I mentioned this to Bev just before Christmas 2016 and we all agreed we would meet up. But Christmas came and went and we had not found the time to make this visit. My spirit team were getting very frustrated with me. "Lynn, you must visit." That is all I kept hearing.

I spoke to Bev again in January and she said, "Right, let's get this booked; there clearly is a reason they want you two to meet."

"I think they want her to help me with my book," I told Bev. I have the feeling it is something to do with what I am writing. Bev managed to get hold of her friend and the date was set; I was going to see Pen on Monday the 13 February. I felt quite nervous really, but I didn't know why. I left for Bev's house on the Sunday as I was staying over there for a catch up before we left the next day to meet her friend. I was excited to be finally going to meet her and I had asked Bev to text her the day before and tell her to bring some items which had belonged to her loved ones, so we could see if I could connect for her.

We set out on the 40-minute journey towards Wakefield in Yorkshire. We were going to meet in a hotel, not at Pen's house, as Pen lived towards Sheffield which was quite a journey. When we arrived, we walked into the hotel through big double doors. "I don't know if she will be here yet," Bev said. "I will try and phone her." Something told me to turn around, and as I did, I heard a lady shout 'hi'. Bev turned around and greeted her friend and we all made our way into the hotel to find somewhere to sit, where it would be quiet and not too many people about. We found the perfect spot, and there was no one else sitting in that area. We ordered tea and started to chat.

Pen was very interested in what I do. "I find it fascinating," she told me. "How long have you been able to connect?"

"Since I was a child, apparently" I replied, smiling. We started talking about my book and what had brought me to write it. She found my story very similar to hers, really.

Pen had been on holiday in Australia. She said the weather was scorching hot and she just couldn't stand to stay outside. She went indoors into the air-conditioning and sat down with her iPad. She told us she didn't know what had come over her; she got this idea for a book and just started writing. Before she knew it, she had written over 60 pages. To quote Pen, "I felt as if someone was behind me pushing for me to write more and more." I found everything she told me to be so interesting and I told her that my story was much the same, except I knew who was doing the pushing.

We decided to order some lunch as we had all been talking for over an hour and a half. Whilst we were waiting for lunch, I asked if she had brought something from any loved ones who had passed. She looked in her bag and pulled out what looked like a belt buckle or a scarf broach. As soon as she placed it in my hand, I felt the spirit of an elderly lady come before me. I asked the lady who she was and she told me she was Mum. I told Pen that I had her mum with me and they passed messages back and forth for a few minutes. I could sense a younger male around her mum also, but I couldn't quite pick up who he was. I am usually quite good on ages of people who have passed, and I sometimes can pick up what they have passed with.

Pen gave me another item to hold, it was a gold ladies watch. That's when a very strange thing happened; I knew this item belonged to a very old lady, but her energy kept bobbing in and out. I couldn't quite understand why. I told Pen that this was an older lady but she was showing herself to me in quite a strange way. I felt as if she kept coming in and out of the room and wouldn't keep still. I felt as if she was also a mum, maybe someone close to Pen had lost their mum. It was at that moment Bev came back to the table. She heard me saying these things to Pen about this lady. Bev realised who I was talking about and said to Pen, "Oh no, I didn't realise she had died."

That's when Pen looked at Bev and said, "She hasn't."

It all made perfect sense now. I had experienced this before, she must be quite ill, I thought, as her soul was coming to me when I called it. Pen told me she was gravely ill with very late stages of Alzheimer's.

"Ah," I said, "that is why she keeps popping in and out." I experienced this before with a lady who came for a reading. Her mum kept coming to me and the girl was getting upset. "She isn't dead," she kept saying but it brought some comfort to know that her mum could escape her body for some relief from the awful Alzheimer disease.

"She has asked me to tell you something, Pen. She says, 'please don't stop coming, I do know you are there, I am locked in that body and cannot respond but I know you come every day and hold my hand'."

Tears filled Pen's eyes. "I only said yesterday, I think we should stop going every day, she doesn't know we are there."

"She must have heard you," I told Pen. "She thanks you for the love and kindness you have shown her."

What an amazing message. we were all brought to tears and it just proves that even when people are at their worst, their souls still escape to some sort of sanity even just for a little while. Within seconds she was gone again. Pen was amazed at all that I had told her and asked if there anyone else about.

"Well," I said, "there have been three people standing behind you this whole time; three, other than your mum and your brother. There is a man and all I can see is fuzzy sticky-out hair. It's as if he has just got out of bed. Flat on the top and sticks out on the sides."

Pen laughed, "That's my dad," she said. Dad gave some messages to Pen; he came across as a very strong man – not much got past him I felt. "Yes, you are right," Pen said, and told me of her dad's character.

"I want to ask you about your book, Pen, if you don't mind."

"No, not at all," she replied.

"Well, we haven't spoken about the story of your book but I would like to tell you a few things before you enlighten me on the unfolding story line."

"Yes, that's fine," she said.

There are two women in your book who I would like to describe, one has dark hair and one is blonde. They are like chalk and cheese, these two women. One is an ordinary working-class woman, and the other looks like she comes from a very wealthy family."

"Wow, you are spot on," Pen replied. "How on earth did you know that?"

"Well," I replied, "you are not going to believe me but they are stood right behind you. They are not fictional, these ladies have actually lived, and you are telling their story." Both Bev and Pen stared at me in amazement.

"I can't believe it," Pen said. "You have them perfectly right."

"They are giving you the details to your book, and they tell me that you are fulfilling their dreams for them. They tell me that your book will be a success and there will be more than one book; there will be three in this series. You will make a lot of money with your writing and there will be more books to come. You are on the right road, continue to move forward and be proud of what you have achieved."

It was right then that I realised it wasn't for my benefit that spirits wanted me to meet Pen, it was for her. The meeting was to help her to realise where this book had come from and to assure her everything was working out in a wonderful way. Spirits had kept me in the dark too. I really thought that I could get some information from the meeting that would help me, instead it was completely the opposite.

I think the punch line for this chapter has to be, God works in mysterious ways.

TWENTY-TWO

My Daughter and her Children

I have spoken many times about my daughter Nicky whilst writing this book. But I have never gone into the depths about the fact that both her children are so very gifted and all have the ability to connect to spirit and are always encouraged to do so.

Sometimes when our children are so small, we watch them playing with their toys and sometimes talking to their imaginary friends, without a care in the world. My grandchildren are no different to anyone else's – the only difference is that they have always been encouraged to speak to spirits if the chance arises. They have never been afraid, nor do they think anything strange about talking to their great granddad whom they have never met in life but only when he visits from heaven to say hello.

I do believe that all children can see their loved ones who have passed and sometimes when encouraged, they can also tell you exactly who they are conversing with. There are many stories of grieving families who tell me that the youngsters or the dog or the cats have been doing strange things in the house. It's as if they are looking at something or someone, I have been told.

This happens all the time and it is the acceptance of this actually happening to you that seems to be more of a problem to everyone.

My grandson Joe, who is now just about to reach his 15th birthday, has had many encounters with his great granddad from spirit. He would sit in his room for hours and talk with his grandfather whilst looking at his books or playing with his toys and Joe didn't think anything strange about it. My dad would have wanted to be a part of his grandchildren's lives and indeed he has.

My daughter has two other children; Brogan who is actually 5 years old today and Jade who is our newest addition – he is 5 months old. Brogan has always been a quiet little girl, very reserved with people she doesn't know, in fact I would tell you that she sees straight through people. She knows if someone is sincere or not. She susses them out in an instant! She has been known to not converse with someone for hours if she isn't sure of them, which is funny because Granddad Ray always jokes that Brogan should have been born with an 'off' switch because she can talk the hind leg off a donkey.

When my daughter was carrying Jade, Brogan's little brother, I know that my father was close by. Nicky was my dad's little blue-eyed girl. I think it was because she lived with them as a tiny child and they did have a strong bond. My daughter has been epileptic all her life and sometimes has been in some dangerous situations when she has fallen and hit her head and there was no one around to help her. My grandchildren have grown up with their mummy's illness and I have to say I am very proud of them. When Joe was little, he would have a redial number on the telephone so that he could contact me if his mummy had fallen. We always called it pinging. Joe would press the phone key and say come quickly, Nanny, Mummy has pinged.

It's amazing how children can adapt to a serious illness when they have to. Brogan is the same; she just takes it in her stride and Nicky tells me that she has even held her hair back for her so she wasn't sick on it, and she will fetch a glass of water for her mummy to drink.

One evening after Brogan had finished her bath, Nicky decided she would quickly jump in whilst Brogan was sitting on the bed reading her school book. She could hear Brogan singing, the alphabet song:

ABCDEFG,HIJKLMNOP,QRSTUV,WXY AND Z
now you know your abc's, you can sing
along with me.

Brogan was singing at the top of her voice and it made Nicky smile, then all of a sudden she heard Brogan say, "Stop it, you're just being silly." Nicky listened to Brogan, quietly wondering who she was talking to. Again, Brogan said with a stern voice, "Stop it, you don't know the words – you're getting it wrong!"

Nicky shouted to Brogan. "Who are you talking to?" Brogan didn't reply but she continued to have the conversation.

"I am not going to help you if you don't listen," Brogan said. "It's not funny," she said and then Brogan started to laugh.

By this time Nicky had got out of the bath and sneaked to the bedroom door. She could see Brogan on the bed, she was staring at the wall. Nicky stepped into the room and asked, "who are you talking to Brogan?"

"I am talking to Granddad Stan," Brogan replied, looking at Nicky as if to say, 'who do you think I am talking to' with a look on her face that would turn you to stone.

"Where is he?" Nicky asked her. Then Brogan pointed to the wall and answered, "He is in heaven, in the stars, silly Mummy."

Dad had told me that he watches over the kids when he can, and he likes to give them some one-on-one when their mummies are busy. "Just because I am over here," he said, "doesn't mean I can't baby-sit now and again."

Brogan knows her grandfather very well and sometimes refers to him as Granddad from the stars; this brings such joy to my daughter and me as we both miss him so very much.

Jade, as I said earlier, is now 5 months old; he is such a lovely little boy, and has proven to me more than once that he also sees the spirit of those loved ones in heaven. I remember the day he was born; I turned up at the hospital to see my new grandson for the very first time. I walked into the room and headed straight for the crib. He was fast asleep, but soon awoke. I was talking to Nicky, checking she was ok; pregnancy is always such a worry with Nicky being epileptic, as she cannot take her meds whilst carrying the baby. This is stressful for everyone around as her health is also important, not just the health of the unborn child. As Nicky's mum, I always worry so much whilst she is pregnant. I know that Nicky is looked after from heaven but it doesn't stop me worrying about her daily.

Jade had heard my voice and as I spent so much time with my daughter whilst she was carrying him, I do think he knew my voice. Straight away, he actually turned his little head towards me and stared straight at me greeting me with his lovely little face. I swear our minds connected at that moment and I heard him say Nanny. Every time I visited from that day on he would react in a strange way. He would stare just above my head, just over my crown and he would make this circle with his mouth, as if he was talking to someone. I know he was seeing my Guardian Angel. She stands proud and tall behind me everywhere I go. Brogan and Ella would tell me that I was gold, 'all gold, Nanny' they would say. I know this was the glow from my angel, as she smiled and made my grandchildren feel comfortable in what they could see.

I do know that people miss out so very much on what is going on around them. How many times has someone said to a child, don't be silly, there is no one there, or your being daft now, I don't want to hear that, or similar stories. It's very sad to me as I know that our loved ones try to communicate with us every day and it's only our minds that close that door so we don't connect like we are more than capable of doing so.

I am hoping that by reading my stories, you too will invite your loved ones in. See the signs and remember, children are born with no hang-ups, they only know truth. If they tell you they are talking to one of your loved ones, they most probably are.

Let spirits into your life; there are wonderful things happening all around you. Know that you are guided on your pathway in life, by your angel and your loved ones.

TWENTY-THREE

Dreams…Are They Real or Imagined?

It was early 4 May 2016, the day before my birthday. I do find it a little odd writing about my husband Ken as I am now remarried to Ray, and have been for nearly 7 years. But when you have loved someone and they have passed, the love returns to you from the heavens and that day was no different.

It was Wednesday evening on the 4May and I had been busy most of the week with readings and healings. I had planned to take the Thursday off completely as the 5May is also Ella's birthday, my granddaughter. I had done an hour-long meditation on the Wednesday evening. It was amazing and I did get a lot of peace from it. Wednesday had been warm and sunny and we were hoping for a nice day for our birthdays the next day.

I had a shower and climbed into bed. I was struggling to get to sleep as I could hear spirits chatting to me. I asked them to shush as I was very tired and had a busy day tomorrow. I always would hear a giggle when I asked them to be quiet and they reminded me that at one point, I wished I could hear them more clearly! "Goodnight Lynn," I heard, then I fell asleep.

I was woken by a very clear dream in the night. First my father had come and sat on my bed; he had come to kiss me on the cheek and wish me a happy birthday. He stayed and chatted for a while, told me what he had been doing and where he had been, asked for me to give his love to the rest of the family and to give Mum a kiss from him. Then he told me goodbye and left. Before he left, he told me that I was to expect another visitor.

I always loved these visits from my dad. When we are asleep, our loved ones can come to visit and our souls can leave us and rise up to meet theirs. Sometimes if I miss them, I call them in just before I go to sleep and I can guarantee you they will be there during the night. When my son's was ill, I would call on my late husband and my dad most nights when I was desperate for some help and some intervention, and they never let me down.

Dad had gone, and my soul had been taken elsewhere, to a special place a special mountain, a place I visit ever year and have done for over 20 years. This place is hidden away in the mountain range of Snowdon in North Wales. The sun was shining and the birds where singing, and there stood Ken, my late husband. "Happy Birthday," he said as he leaned forward and kissed me. "I have brought you a gift," he said. "I have made us a picnic, come sit beside me." We sat on the hill overlooking the lake and Ken talked to me about Chris; he told me how very proud he was of his achievements this year. "He has moved mountains for himself, Lynn. Since his awakening, he has changed his life's pathways. I know it's not been easy for you and your life has taken somewhat of a battering but you too have changed your life. You are heading for wonderful things and I am amazed by what you have achieved," he told me.

I had fought for my child – that is nothing more than any mother would do. I wasn't losing my boy, and I was the only person who could save him and so save him I did. It was so nice to speak with Ken about our son and I know even though Christopher's dad and I didn't always see eye to eye when he was alive, that he would always step in and support me now, when we needed him.

We said our goodbyes and as he turned to walk away he said again, "Happy Birthday, enjoy your day."

I knew I was back in my bed as I could hear the birds outside my window. They were singing away and welcoming a bright new spring morning. I was in and out of sleep still, when I heard the front doorbell; I ran down the hall and answered the front door. There stood the brightest angel I have ever seen. In her hands were a very large bouquet of bright yellow roses; I took them from her and thanked her. She smiled and disappeared.

There was a card attached to the roses, which read, 'I love you still', with two kisses. xx

The very next second I had read the card, the cat jumped onto my bed and I awoke. I realised that I had just dreamt the whole thing. But it felt wonderful to have received these flowers from heaven. I got out of bed and went to the kitchen to make my morning cuppa. I leant over the sink to open the kitchen window and to my complete joy, and believe me they were not there yesterday, there were two bright yellow roses on my rose bush outside. It was only spring and the leaves were not even on the trees properly yet, but there they were proud and beautiful: two bright yellow roses and it was clear to see they were a gift from my loved ones in heaven.

TWENTY-FOUR

My Visit From the Bikers

As I have said, I am visited often from my family 'over the rainbow' as my granddaughter calls it. I have a horsey friend Mandy and she stables her pony on our farm. Her brother-in-law had been here to see Mandy about something but he had not come in his car, he was on his motorbike. The tick tick of the bike reminded me of the days when Ken and I would go out up to Snake Pass in North Wales; how I loved to be on the back of that bike with the wind in my hair and the thrill of the roads, it was just amazing.

I spoke to Steve and told him about my life with motorbikes and told him how I missed it. "Right, that settles it then," he said. "I am heading home to get my spare helmet. You can come with me I am going for a spin up towards Neston."

"Really?" I said very excited.

"Yes, get ready I will be right back." I absolutely loved it; we were out for about 40 minutes and it certainly brought back old memories. He dropped me home and I thanked him.

"Anytime," he said. "Let me know if you want to do it again."

'How very kind of him', I thought. I certainly would love to do it again.

The day moved on and it was time for bed. I lay in bed thinking about my day and about the ride on Steve's motorbike. I must have fallen asleep, but then all of a sudden, I awoke. I was stood in the car park by the lighthouse; I could the put-put of what sounded like a hundred motorbikes. There in front of me was every bike imaginable, Harley Davidson's, Honda Goldwings, racing bikes, every bike ever made was humming in that car park. These bikes gleamed and so did the faces of the men and women sat on them. They were all dressed in bikers' leathers but none of them had on their helmets. One of the men said to me that there was no need for them where they have been. "We can just let the wind blow straight through our hair," he said laughing, and coming from a bald man that was quite funny.

Sat at the front on the most beautiful racing bike was Ken. "Come on," he said. "We are going for a ride." Everywhere was silent except the hum of these great bikes. I could see dog walkers on the top of the hill and cyclists riding past; it was all quite strange. 'Am I awake or am I dreaming'? It all felt so real.

"We are joining the egg run," Ken told me. The egg run is something that happens on the Wirral every Easter and it has done for many years. Thousands of bikers come from all over the country; they bring an Easter gift then, they all head out starting at Forte Perch Rock in New Brighton. They work their way through Wirral delivering these Easter gifts to hospitals and children's homes. This, as I said, is a very old tradition here on the Wirral and the whole area hummed with the sound of the bikes on this Easter Sunday.

I was excited to be joining these bikers for this lovely tradition. I climbed on the bike and we headed off. We joined the back of the big queue of bikes which were leaving in batches. The rush was amazing and it was nearly our turn to leave. It was such a fantastic ride that day, and the crowds waved as we passed by. After the journey ended, the other bikers seemed to just disappear off into the sunset. It was then that Ken brought me back to the lighthouse car park and returned me home safe and sound.

"Thanks so much for taking me with you, I loved every minute of it," I said to him.

"That's ok," he replied.

"Who were all your biker friends?" I asked.

"Well," he said, "those guys loved their bikes as I did but most of them lost their lives whilst riding them. You never forget your roots, Lynn and we all meet every now and again and go for a ride along the places that we loved." I got off the bike and Ken smiled. "See you soon," then he too drove off.

I felt truly blessed to have met these people and thankful for their kindness in letting me be a part of their journey that day.

My dreams are so vivid; I don't class them as dreams – they are most definitely journeys I have taken, or my soul has taken while I sleep.

I want you to take more notice of your dreams as most of the time your loved ones are trying to say hi; they are not gone, they are only a heartbeat away.

TWENTY-FIVE

A Light to Guide Us Home

I have been working with spirits now for many years and I have many clients week in and week out. I am asked many questions from these people, who are seeking answers.

I had a young woman come to me for a reading. she was helped by a friend who stayed with her the whole time she was here. When I took the booking over the phone, one of my guides told me to book her in as soon as possible. "This young woman is in need of your help, Lynn," they told me. So, I did what I was asked and booked her in for the next available appointment.

They were booked for an evening appointment. I prepared my lovely room. I lit the candles as I always do and I blessed the room and called in my guides and the angels. There was a knock at the door; I walked down the hallway to answer only to see something very sad indeed. There stood on my doorstep a lovely young lady and her friend. Her friend was carrying oxygen tanks and stood next to her, was the frailest woman I have ever seen. I greeted them and showed them both down to my room. The young woman, who we shall call Heather, was very slow on her feet and it took her a while to get to the room and sit herself down.

She sat down on my couch and had to catch her breath. I could feel spirits in the room; there were many gathered to help Heather and answer her questions. My guides were talking away to me, as I was asking them what was wrong with her. "Her soul is weak," they told me. "We have worked to bring her to you, Lynn. What she needs from you will help her soul to make the transition and bring her home to God."

"Why would she need me?" I asked. "God will be by her side, won't he?"

"Indeed he is," my guides told me, "but there is something you do not know, you see she was brought up to believe that there is no such place as heaven, that heaven was a fairy tale, and that when you are dead, that is final, you are dead, end of story."

'How very sad,' I thought.

Heather had now caught her breath, well as best as she could, oxygen tank at her side. I felt the presence of two prominent spirits in the room. I greeted them and one of them told me that she was her mother. She was very sad as it was her who had told her daughter that there was no such place as heaven.

"I truly believed this," she told me, "as my family had told me the same thing. It wasn't until I was in my dying hours that my mother came to me, she held out her hand and told me that I was safe and the story I was told as a child was all just that, a story. She took my hand and showed me a glimpse of heaven; I could not believe my eyes," she said.

Of course, I relayed this all back to Heather who was now sat quite close to me; her face was a light, as I described the lady who was talking to me, from spirits. Her hair colour, her eye colour and what she had passed with, I left Heather in no doubt that her mum was standing with us.

Heather took both of my hands and the strangest thing happened. This has only happened a couple of times to me before and one of these times was when my dear friend Lorraine was here for a reading. Heather saw my face change and she could see the face of her mother for a split moment. She held onto my hands tightly, "Tell me, Mum," she said, staring into my eyes, "what is heaven like?"

This was one of the most fascinating moments I have ever experienced. I was still there in the room and still aware of what was happening but it wasn't me talking, it was my voice but the words were not mine. I was channelling from Heather's mum. The emotions were running high for the two of us and there was not a dry eye in the room.

"My beautiful girl, you have been so very ill, but I have been by your side the whole of your life. I have tried so desperately to let you know that your life is not going to end, it is just the beginning. You have struggled with your illness for such a long time, and you know yourself that your heart is weak. I have tried to talk to you, but you couldn't hear me. I asked the Angels to guide you to someone who could help you and here you are. I was so very wrong but I too grew up thinking there was no heaven but there is there really is.

"Let me tell you what I found when I died, my soul was lifted up so very high I could see my own body and everyone around my bed but the pain had all gone, completely gone. I couldn't believe it, I was still me but without the body which was so very broken and in such terrible pain. Nan came for me Heather, she took my hand and within a blink we were in this beautiful place. It was amazing, to describe this to you will not be easy but imagine the brightest of every colour and then make it 100 times brighter. The flowers and trees, the souls of animals just standing around enjoying the sunshine, family and friends standing in line waiting to welcome you back home and most of all the angels drawing you in and showing you the way. There are no words to describe what awaits us when our time on earth is done but know this, my beautiful child, I am here and I am waiting for you to come home, all is well and you will be safe."

It was at that moment I felt myself come back into the room. I was exhausted and tears were rolling down my face I looked at Heather and her friend. They were both staring at me with tears running down their faces.

"I can't believe all that's just happened," her friend said to me. "That was just what Heather needed."

Her mum and grandmother were still with us. "She doesn't have long, Lynn," the grandmother told me. "Please tell her we love her and we will see her soon."

'I can't tell her that'! I thought. I am not telling her she will die soon.

Then my guardian angel touched my face, and I knew everything would be ok. Heather very quietly spoke to me, "They have told me I don't have long to live Lynn. My heart has failed me and there is nothing more that they can do." I stared at her in amazement as she was telling me that she was to die and I didn't have to tell her, which was such a relief. I struggle a lot with that sort of news and it's something I will never get used to.

"Ask my mum to wait for me, it won't be long now."

"She can hear you, Heather," I said.

"What did they say?" she asked me.

"Your grandmother told me to tell you they will stay with you now, and that they love you so very much, and also to tell you, see you soon."

Heather smiled at me. "Now I know you have my gran," she said. "Every conversation I ever had with her, on closing, or putting down the phone, she would say, 'love you, see you soon'."

It was so very hard for me to not sob uncontrollably; in fact I am such a softy, I don't know how I stayed so calm. With my guides and the angels at my side, they helped me to be very strong that evening, and I know I could not have done it without them.

It was time for Heather to leave. We walked to the front door and she turned and hugged me. "Lynn, you will never know what you have done for me tonight. I have lived in worry for many years. You are an angel and a beautiful soul."

I said, "Thank you, how lovely of you to say, but it was spirits not me, you know."

"Indeed it wasn't," she said. "You worked hard to channel my family and when I am gone I promise you this, I will come back and whisper in your ear and you will know I am safe."

She hugged me again and we said our goodbyes.

It was two months later, whilst sitting out on my swing, I heard a voice say, "Thank you Lynn, I am safe." The very next day I had a message from Heather's friend and it read, "I am sorry to tell you that Heather died peacefully in hospital yesterday. Thank you for all you did to help her; she was very brave and was not afraid when she died. I held her hand until the very end. She smiled at me before she died and said, 'Everything is ok, it's amazing'. Then she went home to her mum."

The emotion was so powerful I cried with joy. I think at some time in our lives we have thought about dying and wondered where we would go. I can tell you all this, please don't worry – a beautiful place awaits us all. With our loved ones who have gone before us waiting at those pearly gates, with love in their hearts and a welcoming smile.

But before this happens we have much work to do here. More people like me are needed in this world to spread love and light to every corner. Remember when you enter a room at night and it is so dark you can hardly see, then you reach forward and flick on the switch, the light fills the room and the room is dark no more.

If we stand together and fill the world with love and light, the same thing will happen, love conquers all.

UNTIL WE MEET AGAIN

This is Just the Beginning

This might be the end of this book but it's really only the beginning of my journey and hopefully yours. I have told you nothing of the healings which have turned out to be a miracle from God, I mean actual miracles which have baffled the medical profession.

My work has only just begun. I hope that on reading my book, you are inspired to step out and begin your own journey and learn how to work closely with God and the angels and your guides who are with you daily.

As I finish the last words of this book, my guides have already shown me the next. They have given me the titles to each chapter and I think they are not going to give me much time in-between books.

My new book is called: 'A Little Book of Miracles'.

Within this book I will take you on a journey through some of the most amazing healings and readings, and actual events which have occurred during my life. I will show you just how the spirit world can come in and help you in such inspirational ways. Thank you for being a part of my journey and I wish you love and light for your journey ahead.

ACKNOWLEDGEMENTS

To my mother:
without her, none of this would be possible. She has
provided the constant support and love only a mother
could give.

In memory of my dad:
who was gone too soon. You always encouraged me to
believe, the fairies, the angels and all that others could not
comprehend. I miss you Dad; until we meet again on the
other side.

To my husband:
for his constant encouragement and support, and always
believing in me no matter how crazy I sounded. I couldn't
have done this without you.

To my children:
for the laughter, the pride, and eternal love, and for giving
me my grandchildren who have taught me how far a heart
can expand. The love they have given me is more than any
woman could imagine receiving in one lifetime.

To my dear friend Jon who has stood beside me with every
project and idea, both good and bad over the past years.
His creative talents has produced the beautiful cover
design for my book. He is a true friend and I thank you.

ABOUT THE AUTHOR

Lynn Robinson was born in the 1960s in Wirral, England and grew up like many others in a working-class family. She has overcome many obstacles in her life to bring her to where she is today.

Lynn is a loving wife, mother of three and has one stepson; she has three beautiful granddaughters and two grandsons.

During the years leading up to writing her first book, she worked in the corporate world, and was quite the entrepreneur, but it soon became clear that this was not her pathway forward. Since a very young age, Lynn would communicate and see the angels around her. Lynn set out to discover what these messages meant and how to become closer to the divine spirit and work with the angels. She was guided by spirit for many years and told she would write a book, but had no idea when.

She now teaches a small private class every week of likeminded people, who want to understand what their messages and feelings they are experiencing are about.

In 2016 Lynn sat down and wrote the first of many chapters to her book 'A Light to Guide us Home'. This book sets out Lynn's life story and how her Spirit Guides and her Guardian Angel brought her to where she is today.

Her mission is to help as many people as she can to find the light within themselves and to help them realise that they are not alone and they are guided daily.

---

www.lynn-robinson-medium.co.uk
F: @mediumlynnrobinson